ORCHIDS
AND THEIR CULTIVATION

ORCHIDS
AND THEIR CULTIVATION

DAVID SANDER

BLANDFORD PRESS
POOLE   DORSET

First published 1932

Fourth edition 1954
Fifth edition 1956
Sixth edition 1962
Seventh edition 1969
Eighth edition 1975
Ninth edition 1979

ISBN 0 7137 0979 0

ACKNOWLEDGEMENTS

We are indebted to the late Mr Fred Streeter, V.M.H., for the chapter on hardy orchids; to Mr Rupert Donovan, M.B., late of Clare College, Cambridge, for Fig. 21; to Mr George Fuller formerly of Sanders, St Albans and Kew Gardens, for Figs. 5, 6, 8 and 17; Mr Clive Halls for some of the transparencies for the additional coloured illustrations in this new edition; Mr Norman Parker, one time student at Selsfield Nurseries, for the line drawings; and Peter Hunt of Kew Herbarium for the Orchid Family Chart.

Printed in Great Britain by Tonbridge Printers Ltd,
Peach Hall Works, Tonbridge, Kent

CONTENTS

ALPHABETICAL LIST OF COLOUR PLATES

LIST OF BLACK AND WHITE PLATES

LIST OF LINE DRAWINGS

PREFACE
to the Seventh Edition

ORCHID GROWING as a hobby is becoming more and more popular, though for some unaccountable reason the old fallacies that orchids require special houses, special treatment, and a very 'deep pocket', still largely obtain.

This latest edition of *Orchids and Their Cultivation* is the result of a continued demand for a 'handy book on orchid culture'. This particular edition is rewritten in many parts and has been extended by the additions of several chapters. We have also included many more pictures to make the book of greater interest to the increasing orchid-growing and orchid-minded public.

The chapter on General Culture is followed by a chapter on Specific Cultures of the more important and popular genera. The book will thus be of exceptional interest to those who specialise. We must, however, emphasise that hard-and-fast rules cannot be formulated; outlines only can be indicated. This is because localities vary so much in their environment, and in fact no two greenhouses are exactly alike. There is also the enormous variation in our English climate to allow for—there being hardly two consecutive days with exactly the same temperatures, wind currents, cloud cover, etc.

We hope that this book will help you towards successful orchid culture by indicating the direction, even if we cannot give you the exact path to follow.

With the majority of orchids, their culture is far simpler and less exacting than many other plants in general cultivation, and within limits they will stand more actual neglect. There are no undue difficulties, even for ladies. The materials used in potting are cleaner than ordinary soil and no great exertion is required.

Orchids can be selected in such a manner as to flower at almost any season. Generally speaking, it is the winter flowering types that are in demand from September to May, and the summer flowering ones are much scarcer. This fits into the average picture, for people like to enjoy outdoor gardening during the late spring and summer months.

The complexity of the orchid flower, combined with its delicate shape, and with the intriguing scents, give it a charm which is found in few other families. The longevity of most of the flowers is another factor which makes them very popular. The fact that there are now over 17,000 species in 750 genera known throughout the world and recorded in the several herbaria gives one an idea of the enormous variety that is potentially available. To these species which are, so to speak, God-made, can be added nearly 43,000 hybrids which are listed in *Sanders Orchid Hybrid Lists* dating from 1856 to 1966.

Although many species are now difficult to acquire owing to their scarcity and the enormous costs of collecting, there are, on the other hand, many thousands of popular hybrids available at reasonable prices.

As one grows older one learns more and I like to feel that this, the Seventh Edition of my book, will prove of greater use to the reader than was the previous edition. I should be happy to think that if I could put over to the reader one tenth of what I have learnt in the past five years since the last edition I would have achieved something in revising this book.

Since the last edition there has been what I might term a third revolution in the orchid world. The first revolution took place with the raising of Hybrid Orchids at the turn of the century. The second revolution was undoubtedly started by the scientists who enabled us to reproduce orchids asymbiotically from seed (it is interesting to note that Prof. Burgef is now in his 86th year). The third revolution must undoubtedly be that of the discovery of the possibility of raising orchids by mericlonic culture. This was due entirely to the efforts of a Frenchman called Professor Morel of Versailles Plant Pathological Station. Although the commercial side of mericlonic culture has revolutionised the world, it has also in some respects ruined the old-fashioned business of orchid growing. This in turn has not made it easier for the small commercial orchid grower. Nevertheless, I would like to pay tribute here to Professor Morel and his discovery, which has been so aptly applied by the leading French orchid growers, Vacherot and Lecoufle, and two or three of our English growers.

I am indebted to many friends for commenting on the last edition and suggesting many improvements. In particular do I thank Mr Colin Leakey from Kampala, Uganda, Mr C. B. Dennis of Harrow, Middlesex, and Mr A. Bristow of Eye, Suffolk. Mr Bristow's considerable knowledge of chemistry and proprietary brands of insecticides has made it possible for the chapter on Orchid Pests to read more correctly and, let us hope, until the orchid pests become immune to them, more helpful!

May I wish the readers of this book much enjoyment in this intriguing and unique hobby of orchid growing.

PREFACE
TO THE EIGHTH EDITION

I STAND by all I wrote in the 7th revised edition as to the principles of the general culture of orchids in spite of modern trends. These include, for example, the tendency to change the make-up of composts from time to time according to the availability of materials. Today, the easiest and most generally used compost consists of tree bark and sphagnum peat.

March 1974   David Sander
              Editor 'The Orchid Review' from 1970

PREFACE
TO THE NINTH EDITION

HAVING KNOWN David Sander for many years, indeed he and my father, the late P. R. C. Rittershausen, author of *Successful Orchid Culture* were friends before I was born, it was a great pleasure to be approached by Blandford Press and asked to modernise where necessary his excellent book *Orchids and their Cultivation*.

While making a careful study of his book, I have in no way interferred with the text or style of writing which is so uniquely his own. I have merely changed the names of those orchids which have lately been removed from one genera to another by the botanists, and placed them under the latest generic names, by which they are now more correctly known. I have also been careful to delete certain insecticides which have long since gone out of use and even been banned by the authorities! Otherwise, this, the ninth edition of his book remains wholly as David Sander wrote it and intended it to be read by everyone who has a love of orchids.

October 1978   Wilma Rittershausen
              Editor 'The Orchid Review' from 1979

1

An Introduction to the Orchid Family

~~~~~~~~~~~~~~~~~~~~~~~~~~~~~

WHAT IS an orchid flower? And why is it so readily recognised by anybody? An orchid is, of course, a perfectly normal flowering plant. It is, however, very highly developed and almost comparable in plant life to a highly intelligent scientist in the human realm. The object of all plants on earth is to reproduce themselves by propagation or with the aid of seed. To produce seed a plant must produce a flower or a similar structure involving the two sexes. The art of orchid growing is to induce the plant to produce flowers.

The flower consists basically of nine parts. The elongation of the pedicel, or flower stem, is invariably that part known as the ovary. (This is what is destined eventually to become the seed pod.)

The ovary is twisted in a strange and automatic manner through 180°. This accounts for the labellum of the lip being lowermost and acting as it does as a landing platform for the insect which fertilises that particular flower. This lip, or labellum, is the third petal, the other two petals being superior to it and at an equal angle of 120°. The petals are usually the next most colourful segments of the orchid flower. Behind and outside these three petals are the sepals which protect them when in bud. The sepals, too, are usually coloured, but invariably to a lesser degree. Sometimes the lower sepals are connate (joined together), as with the Slipper Orchid, and sometimes the dorsal sepal (uppermost one) is highly developed and known in the Paphiopedilum as the 'Flag'. Having briefly described those six parts, you will now find it a little more difficult to pick out the remaining three. They consist of a column usually on a line with the ovary, which column has at its tip (outermost end) a beautifully shaped cap covering the pollinia. Orchids do not have

11

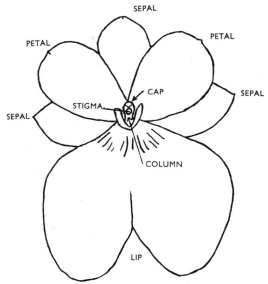

A—Structure of a typical orchid flower (*Monandrae*)
This represents a Miltonia

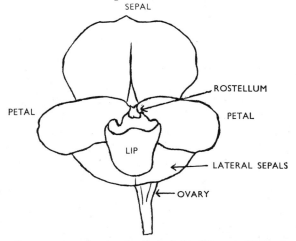

B—Structure of a typical orchid flower (*Diandrae*)
This represents a Cypripedium, more correctly and botanically
known as Paphiopedilum

powdered pollen as a rule, but little sacks of pollen either two, four, six or eight in number. These are attached to the column by a placenta and anthers (usually one). I have described those orchids which are in the vast majority and belong to the section known as *Monandrae*. (There is another section known as *Diandrae* which includes the Paphiopedilum and which have two distinct pollens on separate anthers.) See diagrams A and B below.

Returning to the column, below the cap and pollinia is found a cavity sometimes round, and sometimes shaped like a horizontal slit. This cavity is viscous. It is so shaped as to take pollen only from its own or closely allied genera, and is known as the stigma.

2
History of Orchids

HERE, IN the main, is the address I gave at the third World
Orchid Conference in June 1960, taken from the official report:

Since 1885, when The Royal Horticultural Society held its first
Orchid Conference at South Kensington, very much water has
flowed under the bridge. Some of this water has scintillated with
the reflections of the orchid hybridists the world over. Orchid
culture has, in fact, become a most important hobby for
countless thousands, and 'big business' for quite a number of
people.

At the second Conference, in 1912, the chairman, Mr Gaskell,
whose name is associated with the charming summer-flowering
Cattleya species, expressed his regrets that twenty-seven years
had elapsed since the previous one, and said that he hoped that
the Council of the R.H.S. would hold one annually. Such
conferences have only been held 5 times since Gaskell's day, but
hundreds of shows have been held throughout the world, not
least of which is the annual Chelsea Flower Show, at which
orchids have been exhibited since its inception in May, 1913.

In 1885 some sixty genera of orchids were represented at the
Conference Show and some 350 species. The stress up to the
1920s was on species, and now they are coming back into their
own again. Almost every amateur in the course of the years
experiments with some of them. They may, of course, be grown
perfectly satisfactorily alongside the countless hybrids available
today.

1885 seems a very long time ago, but the papers given at that
conference show that there were some amazingly erudite
speakers. The verbatim reports of the conference speeches
indicate much information both as to genetics and culture. They
were very self-critical. As Dr Melquist suggested in his paper at
the second post-war World Orchid Conference in Honolulu,
orchid growers the world over do not seem to have acted on

advice given in the old days. Orchid hybridisation seems to have remained very much in a rut.

The development of orchids in cultivation since the first species were introduced has followed three distinct phases. Soon after Captain Cook sailed round the world in the first half of the eighteenth century, introducing, as he did, through his botanists, a number of orchids as well as such economic plants as the bread fruit—which were to be used so unfortunately to help feed cheaply the slaves in the West Indies—the East India Company made possible the introduction of many rare plants including orchids which, if of less economic value than bread fruit, did provide an enormous amount of pleasure to a number of amateur orchid growers in this country. Such pioneers as the Calcutta Botanic Gardens collected, classified and grew many hundreds of Indian species and others from farther east.

Among the several very early books which I have enjoyed reading is that of Du Petit Thouars who, in 1828, wrote one of the first works on orchids. His special interest was the Vanilla which had already then become a plant of value to the French Possessions off the African coast. His first work also covers many angraecoids which might arouse some amusement in modern taxonomists! I often wonder if he realised that the Vanilla was in such common use with the Andean civilisations many centuries earlier.

Phase One. This phase, which lasted from 1820 (when the then Kew List covered only thirty-two species) to the end of that century, was a period when countless hundreds of species were introduced and were killed effectively by lack of knowledge of their cultural requirements under glass; and also by slow transport; or, conversely, were grown into most magnificent specimens, as proved by the many Victorian gardening periodicals whose illustrations are well worth consideration. The R.H.S. Floral Committee and, since 1889, the R.H.S. Orchid Committee, have granted an ever increasing number of Awards of Merit and First Class Certificates to specimen plants of species then new to cultivation. Now the pendulum has swung away from orchids and the vast majority of awards are given to hybrids and species other than from the orchid family. One English amateur alone has received many dozens of awards in the last decade for such common plants as *Aechmea fulgens, Cleroden-*

dron balfourii, etc., introduced and cultivated well over half a century ago by just such men as Sander, Low and Veitch. At that time apparently they were not worthy of awards, or possibly the owners had introduced such a medley of species that they did not bother to put them up before the appropriate committee? Thus a modern orchid enthusiast is often 'pipped at the post' as, indeed, I was recently when I showed a truly magnificent plant of *Dendrobium sanderae majus* with seventeen huge white and green flowers. This plant is still in flower after five months. It had received an F.C.C. as long ago as 1903!

Such rarities as *Cattleya dowiana* 'Rosita', *Paphiopedilum rothschildianum, Miltonia roezlii, Coelogyne dayana, Phaius humboldtii, Masdevallia chimaera, Arachnanthe lowii, Anguloa ruckeri, Angraecum sesquipedale, Aerides virens sanderae* were grown into huge, many-flowered specimens during the latter half of this period. The more common orchids, however, which were first popular in this country, were such excellent subjects as *Coelogyne cristata, Cattleya loddigesii,* and *Cattleya skinneri; Cymbidium tracyanum* and *lowianum; Paphiopedilum insigne* and *Dendrobium nobile,* to cite only a few that are still as popular today as they were 150 years ago. In fact, today they still frequently form the basis of beginners' collections.

Who were the people who grew these orchids? Apart from Kew Gardens, and, of course, the Botanic Gardens in both European and tropical countries, there were many hundreds of keen amateur growers. It is impossible in this short paper to list them all, but such names as Cattley, Skinner and Bowring, on the amateur side; and in the trade, such names as Veitch, Low and, later towards the 1860s, Sander, were bywords before 1870. Since that date, as, indeed throughout the golden Victorian age, the names of du Barri Crawshay, Loddiges, Sir Trevor Lawrence, Measures, Gratiot, Godefroy le Boeuf, Graire, Doin, de Lairesse, Lambeau, Van Houtte, Verdonck and Vuylsteke—to mention but very few of the many whose names are perpetuated in the orchids we still grow today—come at once to mind.

Phase Two. Although it was as early as 1856 that the first known man-made orchid was flowered, it was not until well into the 1890s that orchid hybrids and their almost infinite number of clones came into their own. This new period, which I will call

Phase Two, was one in which the orchid hybrid generally took precedence over the species, and the technique of selling orchids was very much changed. In the sales-rooms, for example, a rather dreary succession of tens of thousands of species sold at 2s. 6d., 3s. 6d. and occasionally at 5s. each, was much altered by the inclusion of hybrids which would fetch many guineas, indeed, in one single case, over 1,200 gns. This was for an *Odontoglossum* named after Fred Sander. It was probably a *crispum* hybrid. This phase overlapped the first phase to a certain extent, although the first hybrid Paphiopedilums were available as early as the 1880s. Species were still largely grown, and it was not until the turn of the century and a little after—1902—that the Odontoglossums began to become so popular and so numerous in their many hybrids and clones. These were competed for most avidly by the wealthy amateur.

The climate of growers and their collections changed greatly from now onwards. Whereas the numerous botanic gardens continued the pace with their fine collections of species, the most notable in the British Isles being the Glasnevin Botanic Gardens outside Dublin, the Edinburgh Gardens and, of course, Kew Gardens, most of the larger amateur growers competed in no uncertain manner for the best of all hybrids available. It used to be a question in those days, as many travellers have told me in my younger years, of not upsetting a customer by refusing him a sale. He had frequently to hide a sale to one particular individual from another in the same area.

To my mind this type of rather cheap competition began not only to clutter the 'Orchid Hybrid List' with many hundreds of names, but started a form of rot, continued, alas, into our days. Two, three, and even four genera suffused similarity into a number of new and often unidentifiable hybrids. There were in all of the five popular genera the hybridists worked on very few species apparently considered suitable. The result is that today we have hundreds of Cymbidiums, all looking exactly alike or but slightly different, but under different names derived primarily from only four species. The individuality of the species was soon lost with inter-breeding, and replaced by a show of colour or size of flower which was not infrequently combined with difficulty of culture. The best primary hybrids survived, and many of them have survived until this very day. Their progeny, however, does not often differ from them in the third, fourth and fifth generation.

The collector was virtually dead. The competitive cut-flower merchant was born. The prize was size. A pity, I think, not so much because of the *fact* of hybridisation as the mistake of working on far too few species. We have only to look at the incredible number of anomalous hybrid Dendrobiums pouring into the registrar from Honolulu since 1950, and now from Malaya, all virtually forms of that fine old species, *Dendrobium phalaenopsis* var. *schroederianum* or *veratrifolium,* or perhaps *undulatum.*

The countless Cymbidium hybrids derived as I have already hinted from the four well-known specific prime parents: *iansonii, eburneum, lowianum,* and that wonderful Sander introduction, *insigne,* with an occasional dose of *giganteum,* although this latter species was soon discarded in spite of its having introduced red colour into Cymbidiums. Just occasionally one finds an odd dose of *erythrostylum, grandiflorum* or *tracyanum* blood. The same goes for the Cattleyas where few tyrean-purples have ever surpassed the fine forms of Fabia g. of the 1920s. The fiddle-lipped yellows from *C. bicolor* and *C. aurea* rarely ever exceed the beauty of some of the old Iris clones.

A pity, I repeat, that the second period which saw such men as Alexander produce so many shapely triploid but usually sterile Cymbidiums from that outstanding clone Alexanderi g. 'Westonbirt'; such enthusiasts as the late Mr Lionel de Rothschild, on whose Exbury Estate I was privileged to serve one happy year of my apprenticeship in 1929, and who produced that renowned tetraploid Rosanna g. 'Pinkie'; or MacBean with his fine reds and classic greens; or Sanders—their equally fine second generation *erythrostylum* hybrids such as Early Bird g. 'Pacific' as long ago as in the early 1930s—a pity that their efforts should have been merely acknowledged and not acted on intelligently by most of their successors! That a handful of tetraploids should produce so few better progeny is surprising to me. These were tetraploids which were then not appreciated scientifically as such. The R.H.S. awards to hybrids, so very few in number, prove this.

Baltic g. is perhaps one of the exceptions for this orchid has continued to breed awarded hybrids. So much more could have been done by the introduction of new blood, especially that of unused or little-used species.*

Generally speaking, during the second phase the orchid world was full of self-satisfaction and over commercialisation, and the press, in its usual inimitable way, gave the stress the world over to the insignificant. The one and only truly new 'break' in the genus *Cymbidium* for example, which left the Westonbirt benches (and for a few guineas only) was, I think, a really beautiful miniature named Minuet g. (A.M., R.H.S.). I was delighted to get the plant for Sanders for I was party to the making of that cross with my great friend, the late Stanley Alexander in 1935 or '36. Another similar exception is the unforgettable *Paphiopedilum* Lady Clunas g., whereby hangs a truly remarkable story. Here was a new 'break', a true 'break'— but where is the progeny?

Phase Three is the one in which we live now, and is, I honestly believe, the most promising of the three. Not only have the orchid enthusiasts increased from a mere two or three thousand before the last war (and these were limited almost entirely to Europe and the New England States of the U.S.A.) to well over 15,000 today, but they are distributed, literally, all over the world. This, of course, is in a way quite natural in view of the spread of wealth and the greater industrialisation of many nations. In Britain alone there are well over 3,000 small growers, each usually with only one modest orchid house or mixed plant house and no permanent grower. These most heterogeneous of people are divided up into four distinct types. There are those who collect the better class awarded, or near-award quality hybrids in small but select, intelligently-formed collections. (These will usually part with divisions most profitably.) They are well in the minority. There are those whose enormous range of varieties are grown often in one house, usually with a partition, which have to be seen to be believed. Another very common type of orchid grower is the man who specialises in Cymbidiums and or Paphiopedilums. He chooses the former genus because it requires so very little heat, even in this country, and is therefore an economical proposition and the latter because

---

* The position has since considerably improved. We have new generations of hybrids from new species. For example, *Cymbidium elegans* is now being used, and in *Phalænopsis* there have been most wonderful second and third generation hybrids from the introduction of *Doritis*.

19

of the longevity of their flowers. He also often has at the back of his mind the money that he will make out of his cut flowers which frequently pays the fuel bill. The last group, and I think by far the greatest in this particular country which I know so well, consists of true gardeners who, being typical of all gardeners, have got beyond their perfect green lawns, their well-weeded flowerbeds, their carnations and chrysanthemums, or perhaps their hibiscus, or citrus or pawpaws if they live in the countries where these grow more happily. They just *must* have a shot at orchids—and *do* they succeed!

I have up to now, been speaking mainly of the British Isles. In this third phase I have every reason to believe the centre of interest in orchids, other than Cymbidiums, Paphiopedilums and Odontoglossums, will be found in the States of North America and in the 50th State of the U.S.A., the Hawaiian Islands.

It seems fitting that such charming people as the Kirschs, the Warnes, the Moirs—to mention three only whom I happen to know well—should hie from Honolulu. These three families alone have produced over one hundred *new* bi- and multi-generics in the past twenty years—and what lovely subjects too!

Europe lags far behind with truly new bi- and tri-generic crosses. Of about 200 flowered since 1945, only very few came from Europe. These are 80 per cent American raised! The concentration here in Europe seems to be on Cymbidiums. These are still, I believe, better in quality than those from the Californian, or American, owned Australian stable. In 1960 the actual number of Cymbidiums raised (post-war) were 495 from the U.K. (46 per cent), 463 from the U.S.A. (42 per cent) and 112 from the rest of the world. Paphiopedilums, in which we undoubtedly excel in England, are 70 per cent centred in Britain (1,190 new crosses and only 320, or under 18 per cent from the U.S.A.). The rest of the world accounts for 213, which is approximately 12 per cent. (This in spite of many learned treatises on the subject of chromosomes in relation to breeding which have appeared in the A.O.S. Bulletins.) The position today at the end of 1968, is somewhat different. For example, more Cymbidium hybrids are coming from America than from England. There is a general comprehension of the necessity to introduce new blood and new type of hybrids particularly in the cool-growing sections.

Odontoglossums were, as one would fully expect with such a fine firm as Charlesworth's, centred in Sussex, England. Of 288 crosses raised since the war, 218 are provided from the U.K. and 56 from Europe. America's contribution is 13, and there is one solitary 'other'.

Cattleyas! Here no one will be surprised to hear that of 1,250 raised and registered since the war, no less than 78 per cent come from the U.S.A. Europe, as distinct from the U.K. with 105, produced 136, leaving 41 for all other countries.

May I before I close these, I hope controversial notes which should give subject for some thought, dwell for a moment on *Sanders List of Orchid Hybrids*. After all, given the preponderence of hybrids in culture since the turn of the century, the cultivation of orchids is, in fact, summed up in this list of names!

Since 1952 we, my assistant registrar of orchid hybrids, Mrs J. Wreford, and myself, have spent some 15,000 hours in compiling the new One Table List. The idea was initiated by my cousin, Sam Sander, M.A. He had and has no connection whatsoever with orchids. He also has and had no knowledge whatsoever of the plants themselves. The *Orchid Hybrid List* is to him what it is to many—a list of names. I stress these words advisedly for the register can never be considered a 100 per cent genetic guide.

The two volumes of this work are available direct from our Nursery. Subsequent lists and addenda from 1961 onwards may be obtained direct from the Royal Horticultural Society, London.

The history of orchids is most interestingly described in one of the early chapters of Mr Arthur Swinson's book on my Grandfather entitled *Frederick Sander—the Orchid King*—in fact the whole book consists of the history of orchids, prior to my Grandfather's start, and with special reference to him during the period from 1862.

ORCHIDS IN STONE (See Fig. 22)

Of the ecclesiastical edifices in England the majority date back to pre-Reformation days. The Benedictine Abbey of St Albans is unique in at least one respect. The present Norman structure dating from 1077 was in great part restored in the latter part of the nineteenth century by the late Lord Grimthorpe, including the Lady Chapel until then used as a classroom. The capitals and corbels in this chapel were each carved by a Mr John Baker to represent the 'flowers of Hertfordshire' and finished in 1896. The specimens were collected by a Mr Hulks who was undoubtedly a friend of the late George Moon (illustrator of H. F. C. Sander's magnificent Reichenbachia amongst other works). His sense of humour was not lacking for he introduced at least three exotic orchids, doubtless from Sander's collection, of which Fig. 22 is one—a Cattleya! I had the privilege of rediscovering these 'species' not at the time known even to the then Dean, The Very Rev. C. C. Thicknesse.

Dendrobium leonis

3

General Culture

‹‹‹‹‹‹‹‹‹‹‹‹‹‹‹‹‹‹‹‹‹‹‹‹‹‹‹‹‹‹‹‹‹‹‹

THE LETTERS S (Stove), I (Intermediate), and C (Cool), opposite each plant in the main work refer to the respective greenhouses or divisions most suitable for the plants. The temperatures for these should approximate as follows:

STOVE

During the summer about 70° F. (21° C.) by night, 70–80° F. (21–27° C.) by day, rising higher during sunshine. Winter about 65° F. (18° C.) by night and 70° F. (21° C.) by day.

INTERMEDIATE

During the summer about 65° F. (18° C.) by night and 65–70° F. (18–21° C.) by day, rising higher during sunshine. In winter 55–60° F. (13–16° C.) by night and 60–65° F. (16–18° C.) by day. On sharp, frosty or windy nights the temperature may fall a few degrees provided there is no undue moisture present.

COOL

This division should be kept as near 60° F. (16° C.) as possible by day and night during summer. In winter the night temperature may fall to 50° F. (10° C.) or even less without injury to the plants, but should be increased to 55–60° F. (13–16° C.) during the day if such can be attained without undue pipe heat.

COLD

I have added this section because there are many orchids which come from the mountains of central America and north-east India which can in their natural conditions suffer frost. In greenhouses, with our moisture and more heavily clouded conditions in England, it is not possible to subject any orchid to frost. There are, however, a great number of these Mexican and Indian mountain orchids which will safely go down to 45 and even 40° F. (7–5° C.) during the winter months, provided always that they are kept dry. Most of the types of orchid I have in mind actually need a dry, cool winter rest, e.g., *Cattleya citrina* from the west, and *Dendrobium nobile* from the east. These conditions will also grow Cymbidiums.

The temperatures for such a cold house would go down to 45° F. (7° C.) in the winter months when the plants are dry, but during the rest of the year would be as for the cool house.

At our nursery at Selsfield we have a beginner's orchid house. This house is visited twice a week normally, and that for watering only. In the spring and autumn weeks, however, the blinds are rolled on and off in the morning and evening, at the beginning and end of the days work. It is remarkable how well the plants in this house have grown, and the collection therein is a representative cool house one. The temperature has dropped on a number of occasions to 34° F. (1° C.), (this is not desirable), and regularly throughout the winter to 45° F. (7° C.). The average mean low is a degree or two below 40° F. (5° C.). In the summer months the temperatures have rushed up to as much as 90° F. (32° C.).

The temperatures advised for the cool division apply chiefly to Odontoglossums or the *Odontoglossum crispum* section with the numerous hybrids derived from it. Such plants have what may be termed a soft texture, or comparatively soft fleshy leaves, such as Masdevallias.

On the other hand, there is a large selection of plants termed cool house, which, though they grow well in the temperatures advised, will grow equally well in a house in which the winter temperatures fall occasionally to 40° F. (5° C.) and in summer rise to tropical. Examples are the central American *Odontoglossum grande* or the Burmese high-altitude Dendrobiums and *Vanda coerulea*.

Many of the hard bulbed Oncidiums, Odontoglossums, Lycastes, Cymbidiums, etc., withstand the lower temperature with impunity. It is not, however, desirable to keep the house to this low thermometer reading. Dormant plants are not affected by it, but the atmosphere is too chilly for comfort, and benefit cannot be derived for the plants; better to keep the house with a 'comfortable' feeling, but there are many occasions in our winter when even 50° F. (10° C.) is difficult to maintain in some houses without unduly forcing the pipes, over-heating of which is always fraught with danger to the plants.

For the three divisions the foregoing temperatures must, however, only be regarded as averages. The maximum temperatures may often exceed those given above during the summer, but no attempt should be made to increase the maximums by forcing the heat. In each division, could a chart be made of the temperatures, the ideal would be one delineating an elliptic arc, ascending regularly from January, attaining its maximum in August and falling in a shorter curve to Christmas. The calendar in chapter 14 will give monthly variations.

In practice it is impossible to attain such an ideal and even in their homes plants are subjected to considerable fluctuations. Under glass, temperatures often run up considerably on hot sunny days, but if plenty of moisture and a buoyant atmosphere be maintained, with judicious use of shading, no harm will follow. Extra sun heat is, if anything, beneficial.

The divisions denoted in our catalogue by 'S' 'I' and 'C' to which each orchid should be assigned will be found to give the best results under cultivation. They will not always agree with the temperatures which occur in the habitats of the plants. Quite a number thrive in a moist tropical or semi-tropical summer atmosphere but are the better for a much cooler, drier atmosphere when resting. Probably owing to the more confined atmosphere many orchids succeed better, when cultivated, at a slightly lower temperature than under natural conditions.

HEATING

In studying temperatures, hot water pipes must always be regarded as a necessary evil—necessary because frost, or a damp cold, is death to an orchid under cultivation, but present methods of obtaining artificial temperatures are really antagonistic to all plant life; hence, whenever possible, take full advantage of the sun's warmth to raise temperatures. In winter, particularly during cold windy weather, it is better to have the houses slightly below the given temperature and drier than usual, rather than have the hot water pipes too warm. Hot water piping should always be rather in excess of its requirements so that a genial warmth may be maintained without making the pipes fiercely hot. Nothing is more inimical or productive of insect pests than a dry arid atmosphere in which, as gardeners say, they can 'smell the pipes'.

If possible, control should be had by strong screw-down valves, so that should bright warm days occur in early spring, or even winter, the pipe heat may be lessened or entirely shut off, and the temperature maintained for as long as possible by natural heat. The pipes should seldom be allowed to become so hot as to feel uncomfortable when a hand is kept on them for a minute, hence the advantage of an extra pipe which may or may not be controlled by an extra valve. By giving an extra heating surface, this aids considerably in maintaining temperatures; and will usually be found economical, as a lower temperature of water in say, three pipes, often requires less fuel consumption than to make two pipes radiate the same number of calories. The heating can be by steam, coal, liquid fuel or even electric immersion heaters, but in each case combined with an ample margin of large surfaced piping—better 100 ft of 4 in. pipes at 120° F. (50° C.) surface heat, than 50 ft of 3 in. piping at 200° F. (90° C.).

An excellent contemporary immersion heater is the Humex Heater. It is available in two sizes at a very reasonable charge. It also has a thermostatic control. This is the type we use in our beginner's house. The smaller model will heat 600 cu. ft comfortably for cool-house orchids.

Not satisfied with living with, growing, and generally caring for orchids, sorting and listing them, staging and tying them up and occasionally repotting them—all within the precincts of greenhouses—I decided some two or three years ago that I must have a greenhouse of my own. To be truthful I *had* to buy and build a greenhouse if only because I had been given a most acceptable muscat grape which dated back to the original Roman Vine! So I built, with the help of one of my sons, Peter, a 20-foot house partitioned centrally into two. How to heat it? Having seen many heating systems, most of them rather expensive and bearing in mind the enormous success of electrically heating circulating air, I decided eventually on a Camplex Automatic Space Heater. This is solid, portable and extremely efficient, the fan and other moveable parts being made of some non-rusting plastic material. The casing is strong metal and one can literally stand on the heater. It only requires servicing once a year and this involves a tiny drop of very fine oil and nothing more. The thermostat is probably good but works on a numbered scale which I find very difficult to use effectively. I therefore put in a really good air thermostat in parallel with the fan heater. At the time of writing I have used this fan for three winters and am perfectly satisfied that it is both economical and a great asset to a grower of any plants. Incidentally, I combine my space heater with a radiator which is connected to the house central heating, but this, of course, does not work at nights, being clocked to cut out at 11 p.m. The ideal is to have central heating, if one is lucky enough to possess such a system, to run through to the greenhouse as well. The lagging of pipes from the dwelling-house to the greenhouse is no longer a big problem with modern materials. You may double up—as I have—with an electric space heater to take over when the temperature drops to, say, 50° F. (10° C.) at night.

Electricity and gas are also used for heating small houses, and thermostatic devices render them exceedingly convenient to the amateur. Damage from gas fumes too often arises, and if gas is installed care should be taken that the fumes are carried well away from the house. The drawback to electric tubular heating seems to be the use of pipes of small diameter which quickly become fiercely hot or cold, but excellent results have been obtained from its use, dummy stages being used to correct any undue aridity. Alternatively, an inverted gutter may be used on top of the contact heaters, the gutter being kept full of water. As with hot water heating, it is better to install an excess rather than an under supply of pipes. We shall be pleased to send particulars of an excellent type of basic or supplementary electric heating on request.

A great modern help to the heating of a greenhouse lies in the many plastic materials that are nearly transparent which one can obtain today. THERMOPLUS 50 is an extremely strong, long lasting and washable polythene which I use extensively on my nursery. It most certainly increases the temperature in a green-house for a given amount of fuel by some 5–6° F. (2–3° C.). I recommend it for those greenhouses running north-south where it should be placed on the east side. Always leave an inch space at the ridge and the base so that the air may circulate freely round and prevent the material being quickly overgrown with algae.

It also has the great advantage of enabling an amateur to make a little greenhouse within the greenhouse in which he may keep the temperature much higher simply by the use of a coil of low tension wire. In fact, he builds a frame above the staging in which he places the warmer growing orchids. As much as 10° F. (4–5° C.) extra heat can thus be obtained.

VENTILATION

Because nearly all orchids come from hilly and mountainous countries, fresh air is vital to them and should be freely admitted on all possible occasions, particularly in the cool and intermediate sections. In the stove and East Indian house, so called from the class of orchids grown in it, with its high temperatures, air cannot be so fully given, as harm would result from a lowered temperature. Care must be taken to admit air without causing draughts which are, if anything, more detrimental than fresh air is beneficial.

Again definite rules cannot be given; so much depends upon the position, aspect, structure and means of ventilation in the house. Where a professional gardener or orchid grower is kept, matters are simplified because details are attended to as they arise, but with amateurs, particularly with those who are away from home all day, general rules only can be followed. We sincerely hope the following hints will be found of service, but success will be gained more by common-sense study of the greenhouse, the requirements of the plants, and the weather, than by worrying over rules.

Presupposing that the house is fitted with both top and bottom ventilators, a few experiments, with observation of the wind, will soon show how and when air can be admitted.

Top ventilators should never be opened sufficiently wide or for so long a period as to allow the atmosphere to become dry. On moist days, provided the outside temperature is high enough, top ventilators may be opened throughout the day, especially in the cool section. Whenever a house must be left throughout the day top ventilation may often be given early in the morning, greatly reduced throughout the day and applied again more or less freely during the evening. Bottom ventilators, unless wind is directly impinging on them, may be open all day and reduced more or less at night. In summer both the cool and intermediate sections benefit by top and bottom air at night, but the amount, if any, can only be gauged by observation and an intelligent study of the conditions. The outside temperature and conditions are the governing factors.

An excellent type of ventilation, and one which causes a natural *induction* of air up the walls, along and under the glass, is a 'slot' ventilator at the apex of a house. It is made by having *two* ridge boards, 8–10 in. apart, the capping being raised 2 in. above these parallel ridges by wedges of wood at regular intervals. This is *ideal* for Odontoglossums and other South American mountain species, but perhaps not sufficient for Cymbidiums. An excellent example of this type of ventilation could once be seen at Tunbridge Wells (Messrs. Armstrong & Brown's Nurseries) or in Liège at Sladdens' where can also be seen an ideal mist-spray cooler of simple and cheap construction for Odontoglossums.

In any case top air requires greatest care in its use until the middle of summer. Then more air must be given in the autumn to ensure ripening of the plants and hardening them to withstand the winter. Briefly put, air must be admitted whenever possible, provided that draughts are avoided and temperature and moisture are not unduly affected, both in winter and summer.

Whenever top and bottom ventilators are open at the same time care should be taken that a draught is not caused. Often it will be found advisable to open only the top and bottom ventilators on one (the leeward) side of the house at the same time. Stages, etc., then intervene and prevent direct air currents. Often if the top ventilators are open the atmosphere is benefited if the bottom are kept closed, and vice versa.

In winter top air can practically never be given to the East Indian house and but very seldom to the intermediate. There are many days, unfortunately, in our climate, when all the houses must be kept practically closed.

As a result of having seen several amateur collections of orchids grown to perfection in small greenhouses—I literally mean *small* greenhouses, often only 6 × 8 ft—where the culture was most successfully associated with an electric air fan, I feel I must add the following notes:

It is, to my mind, ideal to have an air extractor in the greenhouse. The position should be at the furthermost point from the door in the apex pane. There will usually be sufficient air drawn in from the cracks around the door to ensure perfect ventilation. The fan should, of course, only come on periodically, either on a clock—say, ten minutes every hour—or alternatively worked in conjunction with a thermostat when the temperatures become too high.

Another excellent system is to push the air through from a preheated room. Here I assume that the entrance to the greenhouse is preceded by a potting-shed or conservatory, or possibly a covered way. The door is then cut in such a manner as to allow a ventilator 5 or 6 in. from the ground, which should be controlled by a slot. In a greenhouse with such equipment I have seen an incredible medley of species, ranging even into some stove-house plants, grown at an average temperature of 60° F. (15–16° C.) *each* plant growing perfectly!

SHADING

This is most convenient in the form of roller blinds made of canvas netting or wooden laths. The latter are perhaps the better as they admit some sunlight but not sufficient to damage the plants. Where possible the laths should be placed running up and down the roof, not horizontally. The sun's rays then play for only a few minutes on any one part of a leaf or plant. Whatever material is used it is better left in position all the year and should be so arranged as to run up and down easily. Blinds are as useful in keeping out the cold on a winter's night as in keeping sun from the plants in summer.

A fine form of shading is provided by the modern plastic woven Blindcloth known as TYGAN T817 which is actually much less expensive than wooden blinds. This fabric is available in 36 in., 48 in. and 60 in. widths. It can be attached to wooden rollers and raised into position by a simple combination of pulleys and nylon rope. I suggest the maximum convenient length of rollers be 10 ft × 2½ in. diameter.

An air space between the glass and the blinds is desirable, especially for cool-house orchids, as this tends to keep a more even temperature in the house and allows a free circulation of air over the outer surface of the glass. It should always be remembered that orchids (with very few exceptions) require and enjoy light and sunlight, but not the sun's direct rays, hence the great superiority of roller blinds over permanent shading. In a climate such as that of Britain, blinds may be wanted but twice in a week in spring and autumn, to prevent the sun's rays injuring the plants. A command, therefore, over the shading is a distinct advantage to the cultivator.

Where it is not desired to fix roller blinds, permanent shading must be.used. Whitewash or any patent preparations, such as Green Summer Cloud, answer the purpose and plants grow well under them, but their disadvantages are that the glass becomes unduly hot under the sun's rays and the house is rendered dull on sunless days.

Blinds should be in position certainly by the end of February or early March and washes, if used, must be applied by then.

If possible delay the application of permanent shading (stippling) till the end of March or even later; use temporary substitutes if available as the tendency of stippling is to make the house slightly gloomy in early morning and in the evenings, or alternatively, stipple but the central half of the panes of glass until April. Wherever stippling is used it should be remembered that such washes break the light but do not tend greatly to prevent heat.

An alternative attended with considerable success is to have small blinds worked on spring pulleys, inside the house, one to each light. A cushion of air, which absorbs and breaks the heat rays of the sun, is thus kept between the glass and the plants, to their advantage. Curtains of very thin material may be tacked on the inside of the roof in early spring and later stippling applied to the outside of the glass instead of outer heavy blinds.

In very sunny positions, blinds and permanent shading (stippling) may be used in conjunction, particularly in the summer.

More shading is required in the spring and early summer. In autumn as much sunlight as possible (watching for the risk of scorching) should be given, combined with air; it is an important factor in ripening the season's growths thus ensuring a flower spike.

Mexican orchids and any with hard pseudo-bulbs, particularly if covered with a membrane, delight in more sunlight than the pseudo-bulbless or softer growthed kinds, and thus should be given a greater amount.

Should any house catch the early morning sun, blinds may, in summer, be left down over night. Alternatively, a screen may be erected some little distance off to break the rays, otherwise the temperature becomes high too early in the day, particularly in the cool division.

Where absence from the house is unavoidable during the day, a certain amount of risk is worth taking during the early spring and autumn, but as the sun gains power leave the blinds down throughout the day. For this reason permanent shading is often preferable for the amateur.

Although in large commercial greenhouses automatic ventilation involves dynamic problems of stress and strain, in the average amateur's greenhouse, let us say up to 30 ft length, an automatic set of blinds is an enormous advantage. Such blinds, if based on light values and intelligently studied for the first few weeks in operation, can prove an absolute boon to an amateur who may be away most of the day at work. The ideal, of course, is the latest type of such automatic blinds which is based on both the light values *and* temperature. I will not go into details, except to state that these really do work.

Of the many transparent plastics available FABLOTHENE 500 is one of the best. This is frequently used these days to increase the warmth in greenhouses and reduce the fuel bill. I mention this plastic material here because it does actually shade the plants as well. One should bear in mind that if such a polythene lining is used in a greenhouse, although it will not affect the flowering of such orchids as Paphiopedilums, it may have a certain deleterious effect on the flowering of Cymbidiums and other bulbous orchids. It is advisable, I think, to leave at least the gable end of the house clear of plastic during the autumn months to allow more direct light in. This part of the house may be covered with plastic less permanently fixed, e.g., held in position by the thin plaster lathes very lightly tacked at the centre and each end. Rarely, if ever, should summer cloud, polythene *and* blinds be used.

DAMPING

In their habitats many orchids grow in positions where always, or during certain seasons, or at certain times of the day, vapour rises from the damp ground or foliage plants beneath them. Much of their nourishment is probably extracted from this vapour, absorbed by their leaves and the aerial roots which so many orchids produce. To imitate these conditions, water is sprayed on the floors, walls and stagings of the houses. The process is known as damping and is very helpful, indeed necessary, to their well-being.

The operation must be performed according to the temperature and the season of the year. All dry corners or odd places should be thoroughly sprayed. Apart from the moisture given off, these places, if neglected, become breeding spots for insects.

It should be understood that a house should not be flooded with water, the greater good results from light but frequent dampings.

The frequency and amount of dampings depends much on the sub-soil. On clay it is unusual for a gardener to need to damp the houses down more than once a day in winter and twice in summer. If the greenhouse is on sandy, light soil it is very probable that it will need damping down three times a day, or, if only two dampings are possible, rather heavier dampings than otherwise. At The Dell★ (Schroeder's collection) one can almost see the pots drying out after damping. This is because the greenhouses are built on a very sandy soil. This is, of course, ideal as the plants delight in being moist and dry alternatively and frequently. It is undoubtedly one of the factors that contributed to the almost perfect culture associated with The Dell until discontinued in recent years.

Pressurised water, which is then virtually oxygenated, is absolutely ideal, and at the same time labour saving. In sixty seconds a 30 ft house can be filled by a fine jet from a common Laycock car washing plant (pressure cleaner).

On hot days a house may require damping three or four times, on dull days once in the morning. In winter, according to the fire heat; once a day may be sufficient in the cool house.

Excepting in the great heat of summer or if undue pipe heat has been used, the warm and intermediate houses hardly require damping in the late afternoon or evening, but the times can only be regulated by observation.

None of the divisions should be unduly moist in the early mornings. In autumn and winter the warm and intermediate divisions should then be on the dry side, but never aridly so.

★ Englefield Green, Surrey, England.

Damping in winter should be done with a rising temperature. Our climate is so variable that the operation must be left entirely to discretion in the dull months. Rarely is it safe in the mid-winter months to damp after midday.

WATERING

This is perhaps the most tricky of the artificial cultural performances required of a grower. Use rain water with the chill taken off. Tap water may also be used in many parts of the country, but should be avoided if the water is heavily chlorinated or contains a large amount of chalk, as for example in Hertfordshire and parts of Surrey, Kent and Sussex. Tap water, even if chlorinated, is preferable to rain water which has in any way been contaminated by tar oils. Tar, creosote, and other similar products are fatal to orchids even in very small doses. Water well when watering at all. Never water a wet plant: waterlogging is undoubtedly the cause of most unsuccessful cultures. Equally important is not to let a plant get paper-dry, unless in certain sections where a dry hard rest is essential for a short period (4 to 8 weeks) to ensure flowering.

Dipping the whole pot in a pail is perhaps the ideal way of watering certain bulbous orchids, such as Dendrobiums. They are usually bone dry after the winter rest. By dipping the plants one ensures that all the air is expelled from the root ball. Dendrobiums should be so watered *throughout* the year. The extraordinary difference in size of bulbs thus produced will repay you amply for the extra effort.

The need for the watering of plants can only be determined by observation, the condition and the nature of the plants. It must be remembered that many species—and hybrids more or less follow their parents—are at certain seasons deluged with rain, hence broadly speaking, all orchids may be heavily and frequently watered *when in full root action*. The appearance of new healthy roots is a sign that water may be given with frequency, if drainage is good.

Pseudo-bulbless varieties, such as Paphiopedilums and Masdevallias require watering throughout the seasons but naturally less frequently in dull weather—perhaps only once every 10–14 days.

Pipe heating is a serious factor to be taken into account when watering plants. Frequently in the winter when one anticipates heavy frost or icy winds at night the tendency is to raise the pipe heat considerably. This dries out the atmosphere and Paphiopedilums in particular must be watched and perhaps watered every three or four days in such weather.

With careful damping and thought as to the season of the year and the condition of the plants as to growth, watering is but little trouble. If the plants are rooting freely, err on the liberal side, but if the plants are dormant water infrequently; whenever water is given soak the compost. When the plants are not rooting or growing, err, if at all, on the dry side.

The term overwatering is often used by professionals. Too much water can hardly be given to a plant when water is required by it. It really means too *frequent* waterings, especially at the time when the particular plant is resting, i.e., growths and roots are dormant (usually in the winter). The result of over-watering is that the old roots decay and are not renewed, and the compost becomes stale and covered with close-growing mosses which prevent aeration.

Water cans with long nozzles are ideal. If you must use a centrifugal pump, let it be the type whereby the flow can be controlled at will at the jet end. A fast flow, or a continuous one, defies the best gardener who then tends to soak indiscriminately plants that need no water that day.

SYRINGING AND SPRAYING

This is a difficult matter on which to give definite ruling. Many growers use the syringe freely during warm weather and benefit the plants under their charge. Properly used, there can be no doubt of the beneficial results that accrue. Odontoglossums undoubtedly are helped on warm days as the whole atmosphere can be cooled and freshened by the syringe. On the other hand much harm can be done by its injudicious or too heavy use. Young growths and sheathing membranes may be surcharged with moisture and the flower spikes within them decay in consequence.

Spraying should be practised rather than syringing, and in any case not too late in the day, so that any superfluous moisture may be dried from the plants by night.

In nature the greatest moisture is usually present in the early morning and is absorbed by the sun's rays. Under cultivation spraying with a syringe or automatic machine may be practised during the warm weather preferably in the morning and afternoon, but always with consideration to the immediate weather. Leaves often receive damage by large drops of water lodging on them and acting as a focus to the sun's rays. Flaws in the glass have the same effect; careful shading is the preventative.

Plicate-leaved plants such as Calanthes, Phaius, Pleiones, Anguloas and Lycastes should never be syringed until the foliage is matured—the infolded leaves are susceptible to damp—nor should any of the membranes or sheaths on Cattleyas and similar plants be allowed to become full of moisture. Plants like Cymbidiums and Paphiopedilums delight in a comparatively heavy syringing in hot weather. With Vandas and vandacious orchids great care should be taken not to spray them too heavily or so late in the day that water lodges in the distichous leaf joints after dark. This would tend to rot potential flower spikes and new growth.

Here again a pressurised pump can atomise water to fall evenly in any required density, and is greatly beneficial. (See under 'Damping'.)

RESTING

In many localities, from which orchids are obtained, the seasons are well and often sharply defined. Torrential rains may be abruptly terminated by dry weather; orchids obtained from those districts are adapted to withstand extremes and to a great extent have become analagous to bulbs in their nature. Many Cattleyas, Epidendrums, Laelias, Oncidiums, Dendrobiums, Calanthes, etc., exhibit well-defined pseudo-bulbs (false bulbs) which act as food reservoirs, conserving moisture and nourishment as do true bulbs, and as in most instances these pseudo-bulbs spring from a common rhizome, extending and forming a new growth which eventually flowers and matures, the young growth can and does obtain much of its vigour from all healthy pseudo-bulbs behind it.

Terrestrial orchids often develop underground tubers or thick tuber-like roots answering the same purpose.

Again, other pseudo-bulbless orchids, Ærides, Angraecums, Saccolabiums, Vandas, etc., show by their stout, coriaceous or terete foliage that they can subsist without water for considerable periods. Even such genera as Masdevallia and Paphiopedilums are possibly subjected to occasional droughts in their habitats and though the foliage is ruined, if the drought be too prolonged, growths are again produced from their rhizomes.

In nature, during such hot and dry, or cold and dry periods, the plants simply exist on their conserved nutriment. Neither roots nor growths are active, the whole plant being quiescent; but possibly heavy dews and moisture—certainly so in some localities—help to maintain vigour in the plant.

Before so many hybrids were raised and cultivated, resting an orchid was a recognised practice by cultivators, every endeavour being made to grow the plants so that their dormant season concurred with our winter and dull season. The plants thus obtained full advantage from our summer and autumn weather.

With young hybrids, often growing through all seasons of the year, the practice has, unfortunately to the detriment of larger plants, lapsed considerably. The resting season of a hybrid is often at variance with that of its parents. By being kept and treated with the growing plants the larger, mature parents tend to produce premature growths and ultimate exhaustion results.

Hybrids which have attained their full size and vigour require rest as do their parents and, though their dormant season may not endure as long as that of some species, they will undoubtedly benefit by similar treatment, modified as to length and season, according to the requirements of the individual plant.

A resting house or division should be an adjunct of any large collection and to it any hard bulbed orchid can be removed after growth has matured. There, with more light and air, a slightly lower temperature, a rather drier atmosphere, fewer dampings and only occasional waterings, it should remain until signs of growths are seen. It will be noticed that occasional waterings are advocated. Conditions under glass are not quite similar to those in the open and the evil of hot water pipes has to be combated, hence occasional soakings will be found beneficial, but in each case the grower must be guided by the state of the plant, and the condition of the house. Exposed to a drought too prolonged, or too much dry heat, the plant may shrivel unduly, and this should be avoided. Such a rest house is not usually available to an amateur orchid grower, but shelves judiciously placed near the glass and at the gable end of the greenhouse or on a lean-to greenhouse wall, provide an excellent means of resting a plant.

Equally possible is it to make a frame within the greenhouse, or to partition off a section for younger plants which are more or less continuously in growth. A few vertical joists of wood and a double lining of polythene will make an excellent frame above the staging.

When young growths are present in winter on intermediate and stove-division inmates, such plants should be given, if possible, a little more warmth, and water must be very carefully administered until root action begins.

For Cattleyas, Epidendrums and similar plants the temperature should never be raised by pipe heat to more than 60° F. (15–16° C.) during the resting period, but exception must be made with the warm growing species, such as *Cattleya lawrenceana*.

Where a separate resting house is not possible and a mixed collection is grown, much may be done by intelligent 'dodging'. Usually one end of the house is cooler than the other, one place gets a little more sunlight, and the larger plants can be removed to such positions and water withheld, or the smaller can be suspended near the glass or placed on convenient shelves.

In the cool house most of the Oncidiums can be so rested. Odontoglossums with one or two exceptions need never be rested in the same sense as advised for Cattleyas, etc.

The resting treatment of tuberous-rooted orchids—as with the bulbous forms—depends on the climatic conditions of their habitats. African species would in general require a dry period, but *Disa grandiflora* must be damp at all times.

In resting plants no rule can be given as to the frequency, or rather infrequency, of the waterings. The plant should be studied and if the foliage shows any inclination to flaccidity or the leading bulbs extreme shrivelling, water should be given.

After a year or so's experience of orchid growing the average intelligent amateur will find that the plant actually speaks for itself, if not aloud, at least by very visible means. A flaccid Paphiopedilum leaf will prompt the eye and the hand to check on a dry root ball.

EPIPHYTAL TREES

Most plantsmen in the course of their lives will have visited

Kew Gardens. Apart from the enormous value to the botanical world of the 7 million dried (or bottled) specimens of species from the world over, the range covers a collection of many thousands of Orchid species and hybrids. Two Orchid houses are open to the public.

In one of these houses you will see a most beautiful arrangement of 'jungle' trees and rocks, beds and pillars of climbing Vandas. You could imitate this and I have indeed a number of amateurs whom I have helped to 'people trees with orchids'. It is great fun. The best way is undoubtedly the 'Kew' way, although the line of least resistance is that whereby one appropriates a dead hard-wood well branched tree trunk, chosen to fit in the gable end of the greenhouse. I find dead may trees, or the lighter branches of an oak—preferably lichen-covered—the most suitable.

Mr Rawlings, the head of the Orchid Department in Kew, devised a wonderful way of creating the jungle epiphytic orchid tree. He used a mixture of peat and cement within and around rabbit wire metal rods to the shape of a tree. By impacting this mixture foot by foot within the wire meshing he has created many naturalistic effects. These set pieces covered in orchids and bromiliads looked wonderfully established after only a couple of years.

POTTING

The best time to pot any orchid is just as root action commences. If possible before the roots actually appear, but in any case as soon as they are seen; injury to young fleshy roots is then avoided. Whenever possible potting should be done in the early spring months as plants then have the benefit of some months of growing weather. Determinate rules cannot be given; everything depends on the individual plant, its state of health, compost, etc.

Never pot during the months of December and January unless absolutely essential. Wait until the days are really lengthening, and begin in February with your Paphiopedilums.

Paphiopedilums may be potted in the later winter months after flowering. It will be noticed that Cattleyas usually have two rooting periods—one early in the season just as the new growth appears and again later from that growth when nearing maturity.

If possible the earlier occasion should be chosen, as by so doing two sets of new roots can enter the compost.

Pine bark chippings are the basis to all good composts. Its lasting qualities make it economical and coarser grades mixed with sphagnum peat render it more suitable for all stronger rooting kinds. For finer rooting plants, Masdevallias, Odontoglossums, etc., a finer grade is suitable and so may be regarded as a good base for all composts.

Used on its own, bark becomes a very dry compost. It is therefore desirable to add a small percentage of medium grade sphagnum peat which retains extra moisture for the plants.

To composts for some of the terrestrial and semi-terrestrial orchids such as Paphiopedilums, Cymbidiums, Phaius, etc., must be added good quality rich fibrous loam carefully sifted.

Orchids need not be potted every year provided the compost remains sweet and good and the pot is large enough to allow growths to expand. Every orchid should be overhauled and re-potted or resurfaced every second year.

Never use too large a pot. With the exception of Cymbidiums, Phaius and a few large fleshy-rooting terrestrial or semi-terrestrial kinds, the smaller the pot the better, provided the plant has room to grow. For this reason Cattleyas, Odontoglossums and plants which similarly grow forward should have the oldest bulb placed near to and touching the back of the pot so that the growing point has the greatest space between it and the front pot edge. Such upward growing single stemmed orchids as Vandas, etc., should, however, be placed in the centre of the pots.

Many scandent growing orchids, such as *Coelogyne pandurata, Eulophiella elizabethiae, Odontoglossum coronarium,* some Oncidiums, etc., are better if placed on rafts, which may be extended as required, while ascending plants such as *Oncidium flexuosum, Zygopetalum maxillare,* are better accommodated by fixing the end of a narrow raft or board of suitable length, in a pot, placing the base of the plant in the pot and inclining it towards and on the raft or board. As such plants grow old they may be either shortened basally or the rafts lengthened.

Baskets made out of teak preferably, or cedar wood, may be used to great advantage for many orchids, including those of scandent and rambling habit which can be twisted into the basket as they grow forward and pinned down with copper wire. There

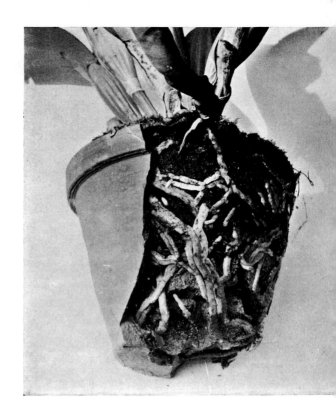

Fig. 1—Portrays a root-bound plant which must have been correctly potted, as roots penetrate evenly throughout compost, and the new growth has started well due to ample root action.

Fig. 2—The author when in business at his Selsfield, Sussex, nurseries preparing a plant for exhibition.

FIG. 3—Automatic under-bench damping at Selsfield. Note overhead spray system.

FIG. 4—High concentration of plants on tiered benches.

FIG. 5—*Paphiopedilum callosum*. Note the warts on the petals.

Fig. 6—*Paphiopedilum godefroyae*—a rare Eastern species.

FIG. 7—*Cattleya* 'Bow Bells'. Perhaps the best-known white English Cattleya.

-*Stanhopea tigrina*, a truly magnificent huge
xy gold and blood-red blotched pungently
flower.

Fig. 9—*Anguioa ciowesii*, the 'Baby in the Cradle'
orchid, the leg-like lobes of the lip moving jerkily
like the legs of a babe.

Fig. 10—A huge Cymbidium pod estimated to contain about two million seeds.

Fig. 11—*Calanthe Harrisii*. A popular Christmas flower.

FIG. 12—*Aerides sanderianum.*

FIG. 13—Showing the beautifully balanced heavy textured rose magenta flushed lower petal or labellum of *Aerides sanderianum.*

FIG. 14—The pure white free-flowering cool-house *Coelogyne cristata* (India).

FIG. 15—*Cymbidium* Pauwelsii—showing the profusion of growth in flowers which can stem from **one small** plant in a few years.

FIG. 16—*Dendrobium phalaenopsis* var. *Schoderianum*. A beautiful amethyst coloured tropical species from the Far East.

FIG. 17—*Aerangis articulata*. A very rare and exquisite species from Africa.

Fig. 18—Admiring a Premier Award exhibit at the Southport Show.

Fig. 19—*Odontonia* Amphia Vanguard.

FIG. 20—The Sander Cup designed by Sir Alfred Gilbert, M.V.O., perhaps better known as the designer of 'Eros' in Piccadilly Circus, London

FIG. 21—Collecting Coryanthes (Bucket Orchid) in the savannahs of Guyana.

Fig. 22—A beautifully carved Cattleya in the Lady Chapel, St Albans Abbey.

Fig. 23—*Coryanthes macrantha*. The 'Bucket Orchid'.

Fig. 24—The author in his laboratory at Selsfield.

is little more beautiful than a well-grown orchid in a basket. The basket also has the advantage of being more easily moved and suspended at various distances from the glass. The only disadvantage is that the plants should really be dipped in a tank rather than watered from above. The extra work involved is amply repaid by the beauty of the plant in this much more natural-looking container. It is of course particularly useful to use baskets for those orchids which require a long, dry winter rest.

Odontoglossums are usually better potted in September or March, as the plants are then more or less rooted into the compost before the extremes of heat and cold.

The following are good general composts:
Nos.

1. For Cattleyas, Laelias, Dendrobiums and coarser rooting Oncidiums: 3 parts medium bark, 1 part sphagnum peat.

2. For seedling Cattleyas, Odontoglossums and finer rooting Oncidiums such as *varicosum, ornithorhynchum,* etc., and small growing genera such as Bulbophyllums: the same proportions as for fresh moss and osmunda fibre in a 50:50 proportion, adding a little peat for the Odontoglossums. Odontoglossums when mature, or seedlings from their third year on, thrive best in 2 parts osmunda, 2 parts moss, 1 part peat and 1 part plastic chips.

3. For Paphiopedilums, with mottled leaves: 2 parts osmunda, and 2 parts sphagnum

4. For Paphiopedilums, green leafed, and Cymbidiums: 2 parts chopped osmunda fibre used with dust, 2 parts cornish grit, 1 part plastic chips, 2 parts slightly chopped moss, 2 parts polypropylene grit, 2 parts sphagnum peat, 1 part charcoal. Add a 3 in. pot of crushed bone meal per bushel.

5. For Calanthes (deciduous), Phaius, Thunias, Pleiones, etc.: 4 parts fibrous loam, 1 part sand, 1 part leafmould and sphagnum.

41

6. For Ærides, Vandas and other vandaceous orchids such as Saccolabiums, Renantheras, etc.: 2 parts coarse bark, 2 parts sieved old compost, 1 part charcoal, 1 part sphagnum peat. This mixture is excellent for imported rootless plants and for sick plants.

It is very important to soak plants well before staging when they are potted in these open composts (i.e. Compost No. 6).

To all the above composts may be advantageously added one part of bracken leaf, rubbed through a ¼ in. sieve. This tends to keep the compost open and sweet.

To all composts potsherds broken to dust and very small pieces, and a little charcoal may be added.

It is usual to place a few lumps of broken bone or hoof and horn above the crocks before potting Cymbidiums and other gross-feeding orchids.

Similarly, it is usual to place lumps of lime broken to a ¼ and ½ in. on the top of the crocks before potting those orchids that require lime such as *Paphiopedilum bellatulum, niveum, concolor,* etc.

The actual operation of potting, though simple, is difficult to describe without demonstration. The better way to learn is to visit an orchid nursery or obtain a practical lesson from an expert.

POTTING PROCEDURE

Select the plant that most requires repotting (leading bulbs right over the pot rim) or that which is about to begin root action. A multiple swelling at the base of the new bulb can often be spotted immediately prior to the roots breaking through: this is the *ideal* time to pot. If the plant has a number of leafless back bulbs, perhaps browned or soft, cut and throw them away.

The plant may be a valuable variety or, for sentimental reasons, you may wish to propagate it vegetatively. If so, a clean cut should be made of those back bulbs which can be removed without endangering the leading portion of the plant. About four bulbs is an essential minimum to ensure flowering. This operation is best done a couple of months before potting.

Prise the plant out of the pot with penknife, working from the back to avoid damaging new growths. You should have already prepared a suitable container (preferably three-quarter plastic or clay pot, unless a teak basket is being used) by placing crocks or rubble at the base over the aperture. Enlarge this aperture, if it be less than ½ in. across, to ensure perfect drainage.

Grasp the plant firmly by the pseudo-bulbs with your left hand, and with potting stick in the right hand scrape downwards from the rhizome into the compost, removing all the soured used material, which should easily fall away.

Now cut the decayed and rotted roots back to the rhizome (base of plant) or to that point where the root appears to be solid and alive. In the case of vigorous young roots cut back to 5 or 6 in. in order to avoid excessive bruising during the potting. Wrap these foreshortened roots round some of the finer compost, working the whole underneath the centre of the plant. Before placing the plant in its new receptacle, cast a few odd fragments of compost over the crocks should you anticipate bruising of the exposed roots.

Now place the plant with the back portion as close to the back rim of the pot as is possible. This should be done in such a manner as to allow at least 1 in. for a three-year-old; 2 in. for a four- to five-year-old, and even up to 3 in. space in front of the leading bulb for a specimen plant. At this point we would stress: *never* over-pot an orchid, rather make the mistake of under-potting.

Next pick up portions of compost with your right hand, pressing the plant firmly against the back rim of the pot with your left hand, taking care when so doing to keep the rhizome level with the rim of the pot, or humped above the rim of the pot. With the right hand now insert fairly large handfuls of compost, with the fingers, pressing inwards and slightly downwards, and filling the bottom half of the receptacle. The plant should now—with any luck—stand up in the pot.

Repeat this in such a manner and with such sized pieces of compost as to allow 1½–2 in, of space to remain below the pot rim.

At this stage stop potting and pick up the plant by its bulbs or leaves. The plant should be so firmly potted that it should not come away from the receptacle. If it does come away, the consistency of your lower layer of compost is not right and there must be holes which, at all events, must be avoided. Remember this compost represents roughly the bark of a tree.

Now repeat this action with slightly smaller handfuls of compost, but this time start in front of the leading bulb and work round first to the right and then to the left, or *vice versa*.

Next insert a pointed bamboo cane close to the rhizome in such a manner that, with the aid of raffia, the leafed bulbs can be tied up. Take care not to insert can close to a new growth (an eye bud).

If you have potted your plant homogeneously, smoothly, firmly and even hardly (in the case of Cattleyas and allied genera) and chosen your time well (in spring if possible), you should, within a month or two, if you break your clay pot, see something like the root action portrayed in Figure 1.

If a plant is putting out beautiful fresh roots in the winter months and you do not think it safe to pot it, it is always possible to break a pot neatly in half and, having firmly fixed the half pot with the aid of a copper wire fast to the rim of the pot in such a manner as to contain the roots, proceed to insert compost carefully around and below the new roots. The plant can usually then be split into two and potted on individually the next year.

How do you split a pot neatly into two equal halves? During the first year of my apprenticeship which was spent at the Mother House at St Albans, more years ago than I care to count, I learnt many useful tips from the older members of the staff. Five members of the Faulkner family were with the firm at that time, and young Will Faulkner (in his late fifties then) in charge of the middle potting shed and a range of houses, taught me much about potting. This is how he would split a pot in two: he would nick the edges of the rim and the bottom at diametrically opposite points with a file. He then filled the pot with wet sand, pressing it down hard and neatly turn it over on to the bench. With a sharp piece of metal—even a large nail—he would then chip the lines between the file points down the slope of the pot, using a small hammer with a staccato action. The pot split into two neat halves nine times out of ten.

DRAINAGE

Drainage is an important factor. Epiphytal orchids should have one-third or more of their pots filled with crocks (broken potsherds) placed more or less upright. If the hole at the bottom of the new pot is small, break it into a larger aperture. Terrestrial and thick rooting kinds, e.g., Paphiopedilums, Cymbidiums, Phaius, etc., require less drainage according to the habit of the plant.

One of the surest ways of impeding quick drainage is by using dusty compost. When potting periodically sieve the compost which tends to get thinner and dustier as the day goes on.

Vandaceous plants which have woody stems which are placed in the centre of the pot, such as Vandas, Ærides, Sarcanthus, Acampe, etc., should have ample drainage. Pieces of potsherd, broken brick or charcoal should be mixed with the compost, in the case of large plants, of the size of a walnut or more.

Cymbidium cochleare

4

Propagation

^^^^^^^^^^^^^^^^^^^^^^^^^^

PROPAGATION, AS opposed to raising from seed, is a technique much more easily performed by an amateur. Most orchids are propagated from back bulbs. These are the bulbs which are usually leafless and have served their purpose being supernumerary to the requirements of the plant. Generally speaking, not less than four and often five bulbs are required to make up a good flowering sized plant whether of Cymbidiums or Cattleyas, or any other bulbous orchid. There are two distinct times when such back bulb propagations may be made. The bulbs may be either severed at the time of propagation, or, much more desirable, they may be cut at the latter end of the year when the plant begins its dormant period, thus usually breaking into growth before the spring. In the case of a Cattleya and the allied genera one can see the live eye at the base of the pseudo-bulb. A V-shaped nick in the rhizome behind the fourth or fifth bulb will suffice to encourage the eye on the next rear bulb to break into growth. In the case of a Cymbidium it is easier to sever the rhizome at the selected point of intersection.

The culture and treatment is different for the two proceedings. For Cymbidium bulbs, for example, usually severed during the potting period, it suffices to put them in pots or pans of sand and peat, preferably with bottom heat. The bulbs are just pushed about a third of their depth into the sand mixture and will with a certain amount of moisture readily break into growth. In the case of Cattleya bulbs thus severed it is best to put them in polythene bags in moss with sufficient moisture (but not visibly liquid) the bags being suspended from the rafters in the light. The alternative is to place a bamboo cane in a pot with fresh sphagnum moss and so fix the severed bulbs that the eye is just below the surface of the moss. When it breaks into growth and begins to root it may be potted up. Similarly the Cymbidiums when they have produced growths some 4–6 in. high and begin root action may be potted up in the smallest possible pot. A Cymbidium bulb which is, let us say, 3–4 in. high and about 2 in. thick should not be placed in a pot larger than 3 in.

The treatment for dividing Paphiopedilums is quite different. This can only be done at the time of potting. When the plant has been prepared for potting, and assuming that the plant has sufficient growths to break into two, one places the thumbs of each hand between the growths which are to be severed and slowly presses them downwards. One can hear the sound of the rhizome cracking and the plant can then be easily divided. Great care should be taken to ensure that the roots are pulled apart slowly, avoiding breaking them off. They are often intermingled in the compost that remains attached to the roots after preparation for potting. Never leave a Paphiopedilum with less than two sturdy growths and a break. The ideal is three or four growths, unless a specimen is to be grown.

For vandaceous orchids there is little that can be done to encourage propagations other than affixing sphagnum moss round the woody stem to induce root action or growth. They do, however, frequently give adventitious growths on the side of the woody stems. Such growths should be left until the first roots appear from the base of them, and when these roots are considered long enough to hold the propagation in a pot, the propagation may be neatly snapped off with the thumb and forefinger. *Vanda suavis* is particularly free with these offsets.

Certain orchids such as Lycastes are very difficult to propagate from back bulbs. They propagate best by severing the *leading* bulb when it is in growth. The main portion of the plant will then usually break into growth again if it is képt sufficiently dry.

I have only dealt with four major genera above, but there are, of course, many other orchids which can be propagated as and when they break and make sufficient leads to justify the removal of parts of the plant, e.g., a Bulbophyllum will frequently break out with two new growths and, in turn, these two growths will make four. After a year or two one of these leading growths together with two or three bulbs behind may be severed and potted up separately. Pleiones propagate themselves very quickly (approximately two and a half times per year). They are unfortunately not typical. Scandent and climbing orchids such as Vanilla and many of the Renantheras may be propagated quite simply by cutting off the upper half of the plant. This should not be done unless there are ample aerial roots to sustain the portion removed. I like to place them against a bamboo cane in a pot with only the lower couple of roots within the compost. It is better to leave as many aerial roots as one can as they are easily bruised if forced into the compost.

To encourage a plant to grow into a specimen it is possible to nick (cut a V section in the rhizome) at various points behind the leading bulbs and growths, thus forcing them to break again. In this manner it is possible in five or six years to make a single leaded Cattleya into a specimen with seven or eight leads. Vandas can often be propagated by 'ringing' the stem and surrounding this incised ringing with sphagnum moss which must be kept moist.

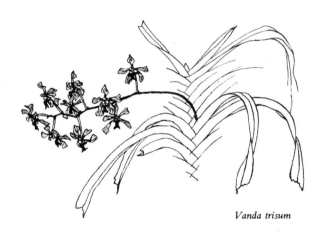

Vanda trisum

5

Meristem Culture

^^^^^^^^^^^^^^^^^^^^^^^^^^^^^^^^

LITTLE DID I realise the opportunity I was missing in 1956, when Professor Morrell wrote me from Versailles concerning Meristem cultures. At the time he let me have some tubes of what were I think protocorms of Coelogyne crossed with Pleione. We had the services of Gerald Rodway (now in charge of the Glasgow University collection of Orchids) who would, I am sure, soon have adapted himself to this wonderful culture had I sent him to Professor Morrell as an apprentice. Unfortunately the old family business was then about to be voluntarily liquidated.

I have little personal experience of the practical side of excising Meristems outside a short day's experimental work at the Glasshouse Crops Research Institute at Littlehampton. It is good to think that in this country there are at least two Englishmen actively engaged in reproducing orchids by Meristem culture, although, most unfortunately, up to now the only orchids that seem to them to be worth mericlonic reproduction are of the genera *Cymbidium, Cattleya, Odontoglossum* and allied plants. The first firm really to do this work seriously under commercial conditions was, of course, Vacherot and Lecoufle of Boissy St. Leger.

What is a Meristem and Meristem culture? Every living growth of a plant has within the tiny bud of a new growth the embryonic leaves and flowers already formed just as an embryonic child is complete in all parts. How are these tiny buds excised—that is, cut out? The growth bud is literally peeled with the use of a scalpel of each successive outer layer until one has reduced it to a very small ½ a millimetre living corm. These are placed aseptically on to suitable liquid nutrient solution sealed in flasks and turned and moved continuously in rotation, usually on a wheel in such a manner as to keep the embryonic nucleus shuffled in the liquid. Within days they seem to produce little

D

nobbly growths and eventually roots. These, in turn, when they are the size of perhaps 5–6 millimetres are dissected into four sections, each with at least one nobbly growth, which in turn are separately rotated making then 16, if the work has been done 100 per cent aseptically, and so on in arithmetical progression to millions! In a few weeks hundreds of these little seedling-like growths will have been produced and can be transplanted into normal flasks. Within a year, theoretically anyway, many 100s of thousands of seedlings may be raised. Each plant being an exact reproduction of the original plant from which the bud growth has been excised.

The whole technique of Meristem Culture is very much more precise and difficult than that of raising orchids from seed. A lot of practice is required and time to separate the original pro-tocorm but it is, nevertheless, a very well worth job *if you want* to have a considerable number of *one* particular orchid. Personally, I think it would be boring to have too many of one orchid, but then I am not a cut-flower merchant and to a cut-flower man it is useful to know that you have got so many hundred plants that will flower on a given day. From an amateur's point of view it does bring down the cost of some of the very expensive clones ('varieties') of hybrids to a figure which is, perhaps, within the reach of their pocket. For example, a really first-class Cym-bidium can now be bought perhaps 2 or 3 inches high for a tenth of the original price.

I have seen a number of Odontonias flowered within eighteen months of starting the process of Meristem Culture. This is, of course, a great advance.

A really full description of Meristems and their culture as against 'shoot tip' culture, appears in the American Orchid Society's Bulletin August 1968 in an excellent article by Walter H. Jessel. A previous article in the February issue, 1966, by Dr. Yoneo Sagawa should also be read, and of course there is other literature available. Do not forget that the original impetus to Meristem culture was with the object in mind of reproducing virus-free plants—in fact carnations in the first place.

There is, however, for the amateur who is really keen another manner of reproducing plants similar to Meristem culture which is known as 'shoot tip' culture, and only involves excising a much larger, and therefore easier, piece of the new live growth aseptically and getting it into a flask onto a normal growing medium. The fingers and hands must be sterilised in the normal way in, for example, Clorox, as also, of course, the scalpel which can be home-made from a chip of a razor blade, in which case it is only used once and then thrown away; the eye having been cut out and held with the forceps is peeled of the outside tissues layer by layer, until a manageable nucleus of leaves which will look like a pale stump perhaps 5 or 6 mm. thick, is obtained and is ready for placing on the usual sterile media as for seed sowing. There is no necessity for agitation. This basic lump will form protocorms which will make plants with roots and when they are larger they may be separated, and again sterilely moved into further flasks where they may be left to grow on until they are some inches high and ready to transplant in the normal way. I say 'in the normal way' but in fact they may be bedded into boxes or pans on a compost of peat, moss or osmunda dust and sand with plenty of drainage, preferably consisting of charcoal. The depth of this compost for these apical propagations should be about 2–3 in. Placed in a warm enough house or frame these young plants will thrive and attain a height of 6–12 in. within eighteen months. I have in mind Cymbidiums. Cattleyas, Odontoglossums and allied genera are more difficult to excise.

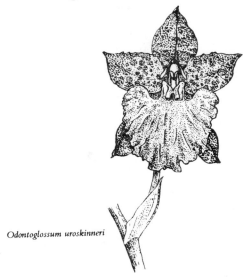

Odontoglossum uroskinneri

6

Specific Cultures

~~~~~~

THE CULTURAL details for Paphiopedilums are much as for Cymbidiums; shading, airing, a moist atmosphere, etc., are similar, but the Paphiopedilums is a soft growing plant with softer leaves, hence it cannot withstand the extremes that Cymbidiums will. Shading should be applied a little earlier if anything and retained a little later. In most parts of the country shading should be in position by mid-February and should not be removed much before the middle of October. The compost should have a larger percentage of bark. Rather more crocks should be used for drainage as Paphiopedilums are impatient of a sodden compost. Re-potting may be done at any time after the flowers are cut. In fact, if a house is available with 60 or 65° F. (15 or 18° C.), the plants may be potted in the winter but, failing that temperature, re-pot in early April.

A marked difference between Paphiopedilums and Cymbidiums is seen in the growth. Paphiopedilums are without pseudo-bulbs and water must be given them as required. In this respect a Cymbidium may be occasionally neglected and the plant will be supported by the stored food, but there are no food stores for Paphiopedilums, which are pseudo-bulbless and the compost should never be allowed to dry out. Never, however, should the compost be water-logged. Should a water-logged plant be found through drip or suchlike calamity, place it immediately on a shelf and dry it out.

In Paphiopedilums, with the exception of *insigne,* species are scarce, but if the house is to be kept cool or moderately cool, then select hyrbids with *insigne* blood in them and avoid all those derived from tropical species (usually mottle-leafed)— *rothschildianum, stonei, callosum, lawrenceanum, curtisii,* etc., unless the *insigne* influence predominates to a large extent. A very charming exception is *Paphiopedilum venustum.* It grows quite cool, preferring somewhere around 50° F. (10° C.).

Usually all Paphiopedilums with mottled foliage required more heat than those with entirely green leaves and, unless a minimum of 60° F. (15–16° C.) is available, should be avoided, but there are a few exceptions in both classes. The chief growing season is from April to end of September and during that period advantage should be taken of natural heat, provided shade and moisture are present. Avoid a draughty arid atmosphere. In summer it is better to give less air by day, and so avoid losing moisture, rather than go to the other extreme for the sake of keeping the house cool but, to compensate, air may be given at night, provided the early morning temperature is at 55° F. (12–13° C.) or only a degree or two lower for a short time.

As with Cymbidiums it is better not to give liquid manure direct to the plants but, from the end of April to the end of September, weak manure water (cow manure or soot are the better) may be thrown on the floors in early evening, a slight smell should be present for an hour or so and the leaves will absorb sufficient from the atmosphere. A small amount of broken bone may be used to advantage at the bottom of the compost.

Thrips, red spider and scale are the chief enemies and a watch should be kept for them, particularly if too much pipe heat has been used, and after hot, dry spells in summer.

CALANTHES

Most Calanthes grown are of the deciduous type that flower in the middle of the winter and are used particularly for cut-flower in the house. The notes that follow apply to them only.

After flowering, the bulbs may remain in their pots in a temperature of 60° F. (15–16° C.) or thereabouts, but in February they should be examined, taken from the pots, the soil removed, and the new bulbs separated from the old ones, all being placed in shallow boxes containing 2–3 in. of sand. Young growths will shortly be seen and, just as the first roots are detected, the bulbs should be potted separately in 5 in. pots, will drained, in a mixture of four parts loam and one part of sand, leafmould and sphagnum peat. Dried cow-manure or sheep droppings, one year old, may also be incorporated.

The bulbs must not be buried, but the soil must be brought up to their base. If necessary, the bulbs may be kept in position by short sticks. There is a tendency for the roots to raise the bulbs slightly and this should be allowed for in potting.

The compost should not be dry, but not wet, as careful watering for the first few weeks is necessary. As the pots become full of roots, water may be freely given and bi-weekly doses of weak liquid manure benefit them. The leaves are plicate and enfolded; while enfolded no water must be allowed to lodge in them, the syringe being entirely withheld from the plants, though it may be used to create a damp atmosphere.

As autumn advances, the leaves will begin to yellow and decay and the plants will not require such frequent waterings. The spikes will not also be seen and, while young, water need not be withheld entirely, but when in flower the plants need not have any.

When growing, Calanthes enjoy a tropical heat. Shading is required, but not heavy. The plants should not fall below 60 or 65° F. (15 or 18° C.) at night and can have a much higher temperature during the day.

The other section of Calanthes includes the charming species *masuca, biloba,* the lovely tall spiked, long lasting white *veratrifolia,* and several others which are not truly deciduous. These are, if anything, more difficult to grow because one simply must not moisten the leaves during the winter months. They should be grown like Phaius. They also, generally speaking, want a fairly warm atmosphere throughout the year, *circa* 60° F. (15–16° C.).

CATTLEYAS

The intermediate houses are often termed the Cattleya Houses, from the predominance of Cattleyas and their allies. The general conditions may be expressed as approaching the tropical in the summer. In autumn more air and light may be given to induce ripening of the summer-made growths. In winter, the temperature should not be less than 55° F. (12–13° C.); damping must be regulated in accordance with the weather and the fire-heat used. Cattleyas and their allies may be freely watered when roots are active, practically throughout the spring, summer, and early autumn but, after the growths are fully developed, waterings should be gradually decreased in frequency and in winter given only to prevent shrivelling of the pseudo-bulbs. From late spring onwards frequent overhead sprayings and syringings are greatly beneficial during growth.

Seedling plants in their own pots from say 2½–4½ in. should be kept growing the whole year round as far as is possible and kept at a temperature as near 60–65° F. (15–18° C.) as possible, with a natural increase by sun heat. They should be potted-on whenever needed—approximately five or six times in 4 years. The smaller or community pan plants must of course be kept under close supervision, and within frames if possible. Do not expose these seedlings to full sunlight between 8 a.m. and 6 p.m. in the summer months.

Although it is impossible to give 100 per cent cultural notes on orchids where the greenhouse conditions, aspect and altitude above sea level, prevailing wind, etc., are not known, the following notes for mature plants and divisions will, we hope, be of considerable help to you.

WINTER (December, January, February)

The plants should be dormant. They should be watered very *in*frequently. Daily 'damping down' of greenhouse should suffice to prevent the bulbs from shrinking. An odd bright sunny day will tend to dry the plants up quickly. Water, therefore, occasionally, *when* plants are dried out. Avoid spraying the plants overhead during these colder months, except on fine warm sunny days.

SPRING (March, April, May)

Having retarded any growth that may have appeared in the winer by withholding water, look out now for those plants that produce new growths. There will be two distinct types of growths. One type will grow almost to maturity before roots appear from the base of the *completed* bulb. This type wants less frequent watering than the second type. The second type will root with the young growth—usually when 3–4 in. up—and requires regular waterings, probably as often as once a week, dependent on atmospheric conditions.

Syringe the plants whenever weather conditions permit. This syringing and overhead spraying will apreciably reduce the number of surface waterings that will be required. *Never* water a wet plant. *Waterlogging* will kill the root action!

Shade the plants from direct sunlight as from mid to end March, according to locality.

55

Potting may begin in May, or even April, the ideal moment being just before root action begins. The root swellings can be seen at the base of the new growth.

SUMMER (June, July, August)

Potting may be continued where necessary. Allow approximately 1–1½ in. in front of the leading bulb for 4-year-old plants. Repotting is not usually required more often than every other year, until the plants become specimens when they may go from three to four years with just a 'top-dressing' in between. By 'top-dressing' is meant a sweetening on the surface by the removal of algae, ferns, foreign growths, etc., and the filling up of holes with fresh bark. The rear bulb should be squeezed well back against the rim of the pot.

Continue watering fairly copiously, spraying and syringing at least twice a day, once in the morning before 10 and once in the afternoon an hour or two before sundown. A short spray midday is beneficial when convenient. Keep atmospheric conditions as near 100 per cent moist as possible.

Shade *heavily* in those three months, at least until mi-August when shading is progressively reduced by washing away part of the 'Summer Cloud', or by rolling back the wooden lathe or roller blinds, later in the morning or earlier in the afternoon on the east and west slopes respectively.

AUTUMN (September, October, November)

Reduce shading to nil during the first month of September. Light is essential to ripen bulbs and flowers. Do not worry if leaves go a little yellowy-green, but never must they go yellow. Bulbs may shrivel a little. This does no harm if they are not allowed to shrivel abjectly.

Reduce watering progressively. The ideal will be the plant that has the matured bulb with flower sheath well forward showing by August!

During these pre-winter months, make sure your plants are clean. Avoid all potting from now until spring. If potting is necessary, pot *on* without disturbing the root ball, rather than repot. This can even be done by a half pot wired to the pot in front of the growth.

TEMPERATURES

For the winter months try to ensure a minimum all night 'low' temperature of 62° F. (16–17° C.). As the plants mature 55–58° F. (12–14° C.) will suffice. By day the temperature should rise to 65–70° F. (18–21° C.) but of course may rise higher by sun heat, providing atmospheric humidity is sufficient (70–80 per cent). In the spring months the night minimum should be slightly raised to 65° F. (18° C.) and by day from 70–75° F. (21–24° C.). Reduce night temperatures to 60° F. (15–16° C.) again as the autumn advances.

FLOWERING

When the buds push through the sheaths, whether summer, autumn or winter, or spring, avoid watering the plant. Avoid over-moist atmosphere conditions. Give maximum amount of light. This will ensure good, clean, perfect, long-lasting blooms, and what is more, prevent the buds from turning yellow and rotting.

One can easily see when the buds begin to push through the sheath by lifting the plant and placing the sheath against the light.

The above notes, of course, apply not only to Cattleyas but to their various hybrids. Generally speaking, the Laeliocattleyas are slightly easier to grow, just as the hybrids with Sophronitis blood in them usually rather more difficult and slower growing, also more reluctant to flower. On the other hand, there are many Sophrocattleya hybrids which flower very freely.

There are a number of Cattleyas, particularly those from the Guianas and Venezuela, which require very much more heat, such as *superba, lawrenceana,* and *dowiana* from Costa Rica. Most growers indicate when a Cattleya does need a higher minimum in the winter. The minimum for these warmer growing Cattleyas should be 65° F. (18° C.).

CYMBIDIUMS

Cymbidiums are essentially the orchid for the amateur. We have known the cool-house temperatures to fall within two degrees of freezing-point and yet plants and flowers remained uninjured, but let 'safety first' be the motto; 45° F. (7° C.) should be regarded as the minimum. Better still, keep the temperature and atmosphere of the house comfortable to yourselves, and the plants will feel equally happy. This means that in winter never

57

attempt to force the temperature much above 50° F. (10° C.) by pipe heat. On many days it will naturally rise higher.

Seedling plants in 1–4 in. pots, and community pans which are best kept within a frame, should be grown a little warmer and shadier than their 'big brother'. 60° F. (15–16° C.) would be ideal, with increases by natural sun–heat. They should also be potted on frequently, in fact every 6 months.

There are no hard and fast rules with their culture. Water is never withheld for any length of time, but naturally waterings are more infrequent during cold, damp weather. Air should be admitted whenever possible, but draughts avoided at all times. Night air may be given whenever the outer temperature safely permits.

There is probably no class of plant which will withstand extremes better, but much greater success is obtained by not subjecting plants to extremes.

Safety lies within a minimum of 45° F. (7° C.) and a maximum of 80° F. (26–27° C.), pipe heat being used as little as possible.

Shading should be in place by the end of February or early March, as it is most necessary in the early spring and summer months. In the autumn it must be lessened, as the plants must be hardened to withstand the winter and direct sunlight then ensures flowering.

For compost, use one part of sphagnum peat or loam fibre, medium bark or crushed bricks may also be incorporated to keep the compost open. An alternative compost may include the addition of one part rubbed beach and oak leaves and bracken. The bracken stalks are not used except the thin axillary ones. This compost is found to keep very sweet for much longer than compost involving loam, however fibrous be the loam.

Cymbidiums have fleshy roots and are heavy feeders so usually require re–potting every two years. A small quantity of bone meal should be added to compost: a 2 in. potful per bushel.

In potting, all dead roots should be cut clean and, if too many healthy roots are present, cut some away and shorten others back. Do not be afraid of cutting them; the thick heavy bulbs will keep the plants going for quite a time. After re–potting do not water for few—three or four—days but, if possible, keep the foliage syringed and the tops of the post damped slightly. Re–potting is better done after flowering, when the growths are at least 3 in. high.

The flower spikes are developed in autumn, but the flowers will not be seen until after Christmas with the exceptions, still rare, of the *erythrostylum* and *tracyanum* early flowering new hybrids. They will last two months or more in bloom. To obtain specimen plants, cut the spikes after they have been open two or three weeks; they will last quite a long time in water. Plants with four or more spikes are far more effective than plants with one.

In addition to the species such as *lowianum, tracyanum, insigne, ballianum, giganteum* and *hookerianum,* there are today over 2,500 different hybrids, all requiring similar treatment and all producing large spikes of long-lasting flowers.

C. eburneum, sinensis, and *finalysonianum* and one or two others like more warmth—an intermediate house culture.

There have been raised in America a number of warmer growing hybrids, which, by the way, we are growing at our Selsfield Nursery. These are mainly raised for amateurs who grow them in warmer climatic conditions, but also may be of use to certain British amateurs who have only a warm house. These hybrids are in the main derived from the Malayan species.

Cymbidiums are sometimes affected by virus which would appear to be inherent in some hybrids. Extra warmth will usually grow them out of it. I believe it to be caused by cold dank conditions, and I know it to be started not infrequently by excessive manuring. It is, however, an indisputable fact that Alexanderi g. 'Westonbirt' invariably has inherent virus which it passes on to many of its progeny. But the latter statement is not a proven fact, though it is a fact that virus may be passed on by the sap. Avoid using your penknife on virused leaves. Remove the leaves rather by splitting the rib down to the bulb and burn them at once. If you use a knife sterilise in alcohol after use. (See also under Virus, pages 90–92.)

Contrary to popular belief, but conforming with the opinion of so-called 'old-fashioned' people, such as the late Mr E. Cooper, A.H., R.H.S., Cymbidiums in order to give a maximum flower spike should be grown in media of a p.H. value of never more than 6.85 and never less than 7.10. These figures are based on a collection where plants averaged over two spikes per bulb and twenty-five flowers per spike.

To dose down acidity, use Calcium nitrates.

BEDDING CYMBIDIUMS

There is such a furore for bedding Cymbidiums now that information may be obtained from almost any nursery. There are, however, some misapprehensions to be contradicted. Many amateurs believe that when they retire they can bed out Cymbidiums in certain quantities and make sufficient profit from their cut flower to pay for the heating and installation as well as the cost of the plant. This is rarely the case. In fact there is tremendous competition on the London and other markets.

Nevertheless, it is satisfying to have a bed of Cymbidiums and hope for a little return to cover if only some of the costs of heating, etc. If this bedding is to be done satisfactorily it is essential that the person building the bed should beware of the following facts:

The bed must be based on a well-drained bottom. This drainage should consist of not less than 4 in. and if possible 6 in. of broken brick and rubble. On top of this may be placed some damper material such as bracken which will prevent the next level of compost from draining through. On top of this should be a layer of charcoal and if possible a fair quantity of large bone chippings and/or hoof and horn. Above this the compost is subject to debate. Generally speaking, I agree that an ideal compost should consist of:

Parts:		Bushels:
3	Sphagnum peat—lumpy NOT powdered ...	6
½	Bone Meal	1
2	Chopped dried and sieved oak and/or beech leaves	4
1	Osmunda fibre	2
¾	Charcoal	1½
¼	Cornish grit or polypropylene	½

This mixture should preferably be sieved through an ½ in. mesh sieve thus removing all dust.

N.B. Rootballs of plants previously grown in pots for more than 1 year *must* be well broken up and decayed matter removed.

DENDROBIUMS

Nearly all the Burmese Dendrobiums: *D. nobile, aggregatum, amoenum, aureum, bensoniae, boxallii, brymerianum, chrysanthum, chrysotoxum, clavatum, crassinode, crepidatum, cretaceum, crystallinum, devonianum, pierardii, primulinum, findlayanum, formosum, lituiflorum, parishii, suavissimum, thyrisflorum,* and *wardianum,* with hybrids from them, can be grown in a tropical atmosphere during summer and rested in a temperature of 50–55° F. (10–12° C.) Give them only very occasional waterings, if any, during resting period.

There are a number of cooler growing Dendrobiums that come from the eastern end of the Himalayas which will suffer lower temperatures such as *nobile, jamesianum,* and from the mountains of Queensland the charming *speciosum,* and *kingianum.* These may rest as low as 45° F. (7° C.) in the winter.

The Far-Eastern Dendrobiums: *D. phalænopis, acuminatum, bigibbum,* as also such Philippine species as *amoenum* and *dearei,* etc., require a stove temperature throughout the year. Strangely enough one of the Philippine Dendrobiums, *victoria-reginae,* is best grown cool as it is found in the rain clouds high up above Manila.

All Dendrobiums should be given as small a receptacle as possible, water may thus be more freely administered during the growing season. Many of the Burmese species commence growth later in winter but, as new roots are not present, such growths do not affect the treatment as regards watering, etc.

D. phalænopis, undulatum and their hard bulbed allies should be given as much light throughout the year as safety permits. I cannot stress sufficiently this factor of light. These hard bulbed types of Dendrobiums are rather more difficult to grow and tend in the winter to lose the new growths, or those that are just completed. They must never be sprayed overhead during these winter months. Perhaps once a month it is safe to dip the plants, taking care not to wet inside the base of the growths. This section of Eastern Dendrobiums should rest with an absolute minimum temperature of 60° F. (15–16° C.). They grow best in temperatures of 65–70° F. (18–21° C.).

ODONTOGLOSSUMS AND ONCIDIUMS

These genera may be divided into two sections as regards culture with, so to speak, connecting links.

Odontoglossum crispum and its hybrids, *O. aspidorrhinum, bictoniense, bladum, cirrhosum, constrictum, coradinei, edwardii, facetum, gloriosum, hallii, harryanum, hystrix, kegelgani, lindley-anum, naevium, nebulosum, nevadense, odoratum, pescatorei, platychilum, sceptrum, tripudians, triumphans,* etc., and Oncidiums of the *Oncidium macranthum* section require throughout the year a cool-moist atmosphere as near 60° F. (15–16° C.) as possible in the summer, not below 50° F. (10° C.) in the winter. They resent pipe heat or any approach to a dry atmosphere. Air must be admitted whenever possible, but draughts must be avoided. Bottom air can often be largely used with advantage. In summer, top air must not be so given by day as to allow too much loss of moisture.

Potting should be effected early in spring or alternatively early in September.

Shading should be in place by February, so that it can be used if required. In autumn, admit more light and air to ripen the plants. Though in winter water is naturally given much less frequently than in summer, it must not be withheld for long intervals. The plants must be studied. If growths are matured, then allow the compost to become moderately dry between the waterings. In other stages of growth, keep the plants moist.

A golden rule is never to water Odontoglossums or damp down when the temperature drops below 50° F. (10° C.); water and damp sparingly when the temperature is as low as 50° F. (10° C.), water and damp freely when the temperature is above 60° F. (15–16° C.).

On warm days, overhead syringing may be freely indulged in, but it is not advisable to allow moisture to remain in the growths overnight. When outside conditions are safe, night air may be freely admitted. Thrips are particularly fond of the flowers and young growths and should be looked for frequently. Attention is specially necessary during the heat of summer and when pipe heat has to be used in winter. It is wise to spray monthly in spring and summer with a suitable insecticide as a preventative measure whether or not you have found thrips present on the leaves.

A second section, in which *O. grande* and *O. citrosmum* may be cited, have harder pseudo-bulbs and foliage. Provided a moist atmosphere with the necessary shading is maintained, they do not mind a much higher temperature in the summer and in the winter are benefited by a very decided rest. Aim at a temperature of 50° F. (10° C.) at night, but occasional falls below that do no harm, as the bulbs should be finished and ripened by late autumn. With *O. grande* may be grown *O. citosmum, insleayii, schlieperianum* and a number of Oncidiums—*tigrinum, aurosum, batemannianum, crispum, gravesianum, praetextum, varicosum,* etc.

Other Odontoglossums— *O. rossii, cervantesii, pulchellum* and Oncidiums like *incurvum, candidum, marshallianum, papilio,* etc., and similar growing kinds, can be grown in the *O. crispum* house, the smaller ones suspended near the glass, but they appreciate a slightly warmer temperature in summer and a slightly drier atmosphere in the winter. Odontiodas and Odontonias can be treated much as *crispum,* with slight variations governed by their parentage and the nature of their pseudo-bulbs and foliage, although Odontonias will thrive in a warmer average temperature (65–68° F.) (18–20° C.).

Some Oncidiums such as *kramerianum, cebolleta, splendidum, carthaginense, roseum, cavendishianum* and others from the coastal and hotter parts of Central America and the West Indies, as also from Southern Mexico and Guatemala, require stove or warm-intermediate houses with minimum temperatures of nearer 60–65° F. (15–18° C.), although they will, unlike Odontoglossums of the *crispum* section, rest drier for a period after growth. In fact, little or no water should be given during the months of November, December and January. There is otherwise a tendency for these fleshy leaved Oncidiums to rot at the base of the leading growths. The leaf bracts will tend to soften and the flower spike within them rot.

MILTONIAS

The appearance of innumerable hybrids and crosses between *M. vexillaria* and *M. roezlii* calls for special mention. The flowers are produced usually in May and summer and their rich varied tints and long duration on the plant entitles them to a deserved popularity.

The plants are amenable to cultivation, but their culture should not be attempted when the minimum winter temperature falls below 55° F. (12–13° C.). Effort should be made to keep a winter temperature of not less than 58° F. (14° C.) because they really require a slightly warmer temperature than that given to the average cool or Odontoglossum house. While they hardly require that necessary to Cattleyas, they nevertheless grow best in a Cattleya or Cypripedium house.

The pots or pans used should be as small as possible, as the plants should be liberally watered when in full growth and root action.

Compost should consist of three parts osmunda fibre, cleaned and cut rather fine, one part of sphagnum moss, with a quarter part of oak or beech leaves, a little sand and crushed charcoal. Potting may be effected in early April or early September. From April keep the plants in a warm buoyant atmosphere, but using as little pipe heat as possible. In warm weather the plants may be syringed freely. Thrips are particularly fond of the flower and flower buds and gentle fumigation or with insecticide should be given as a preventive. If attacked, the plant and flower spikes should be dipped in insecticide solution.

In winter the atmosphere must not be too humid and water must be carefully given, allowing the compost to become moderately dry between waterings. Night air may be admitted with advantage during hot weather but at all times draught must be avoided.

As Miltonias tend to bruise rather easily and will quickly rot in the winter months if thus bruised, avoid handling the plants excessively. On no account must water lodge in the leaf axils or young growths during the winter. One should also take great care to cut off a flower spike just before the flowers drop. A dead flower lying on a leaf below for even as short a period as five or six hours will cause that leaf to mark and rot. The rot tends to spread through the plant. If black marks or black rot marks are noted on the bulbs or leaves, immediately treat them with lime or sulphur.

VANDAS

These orchids, and the closely allied species which are monopodial (i.e., growing upwards) of the same vandaceous habit, are almost continuously in growth.

This interesting genus may be split up for the pupose of these notes into three distinct types. The first section is perhaps the most common and includes the warmer grown strap–leaved species, e.g., *luzonica, sanderiana, tricolor, suavis, insignis, dearei,* etc. These require careful shading throughout the year and a fully saturated atmosphere. If potted correctly in potsherds and brick rubble, loosely, with a superficial surfacing of coarse bark, these

Ceratostylis rubra

Phalaenopsis Princess Rose

Brassia maculata

4 *Chysis bractescens*

5 *Brassavola cordata*

6 *Cymbidium elegans*

7 *Broughtonia sanguinea*

8 *Stenia* sp.

9 *Oncidium pulchellum*

10 *Dendrobium chrysotoxum*

11 *Cochlioda noezliana*

12 *Miltonia roezlii* 'El Valle'

Laelia anceps 'Selsfield'

Laelia gouldiana

Dendrobium phalaenopsis var. schroderianum

16 Eulophiella Rolfei

17 Doritis pulcherrima

18 Lockhartia verrucosa

19 *Pleurothallis dioniae*

20 *Pleurothallis palliolata*

21 *Cirrhopetalum medusae* 'Album'

22 *Platystele ornata*

23 *Paphiopedilum hirsutissimum*

24 *Ascocentrum ampullaceum*

Encyclia mariae

Cochleanthes aromatica

Dendrobium jamesianum

28 Maxillaria splendens

29 Trichopilia coccinea

30 Phaius tancarvilliae

31 *Odontoglossum bictoniense*

32 *Sophronitis coccinea*

33 *Odontoglossum crispum*

34 *Hexisea bidentata*

35 *Pholidota chinensis*

36 *Renanthera imschootiana*

Galeandra devoniana

Brassavola David Sander

Dendrochilum (Platyclinis) filiforme

40 *Cymbidium* Oriental Legend

41 *Miltonia* Goodale Moir

42 *Vanda* Chuan Aik 'Selsfield'

43 *Laeliocattleya* Bonanza

44 *Odontoglossum* Eileen King

45 *Odontonia* Irma La Douce

46 *Odontoglossum* Queen Alexandra

47 *Vuylstekeara* Edna Stamperland

48 *Charlesworthara* Rajah 'Selsfield'

should require but little watering with a can. In spring and summer, however, they must be heavily syringed as frequently as possible. *Sanderiana* and *luzonica* require a temperature that does not fall below 70–75° F. (21–24° C.) and others will support a drop of another 5° F. (3° C.) in the winter.

The parent most used in hybrids today is *Vanda sanderiana.* There have been many hundreds of hybrids raised in the last decade or two in the Hawaiian Islands. They are the most colourful and beautiful perhaps of modern orchid hybrids. They also last a very long while in flower.

We now come to the second section which consists of the terete and semi–terete Vandas. This type is a sun–loving type which has pencil–like leaves with very narrow slits which are particularly prone to scale. The semi–teretes have thick leaves, but are flatter and easier to keep clean. This section includes many lovely hybrids and species and, as said before, requires a great deal of direct light.

We now come to the last and smallest section of cool-growing Vandas, mostly from north–east India, of which *coerulea, kimballiana* and *amesiana* are the most common. These may be rested in a cool-intermediate house during winter and will remain more or less dormant with a winter minimum of from 45–50° F. (7–10° C.). These, of course, require sun heat in summer and during the late summer and autumn months flower all the better for exposure to the direct sun rays.

PHALAENOPSIS

The culture of Phalaenopsis is similar in almost all ways to Vandas and they, too, require considerable temperatures. The great difference between Vandas and Phalaenopsis is that Phalaenopsis like and thrive in shaded light. What they need above all is warmth and there are only a few types which will grow successfully at temperatures as low as 60° F. (15–16° C.). The ideal temperature is nearer 70° F. (21° C.), but in practice one succeeds very well with temperatures that average 65° F. (18° C.).

As is so often the case with orchids, the more resistant types are the species and if you must grow a Phalaenopsis with a temperature that drops to 60° F. (15–16° C.) and slightly lower at night, then I suggest you choose *P. stuartiana* or *amabilis,* some of which can be grown most successfully with 58° F. (14–15° C.) minimum. There are various types of *amabilis* and much depends on the type you obtain and where it came from. Plenty of shade and plenty of heat—those are the secrets for successful culture which is rewarded with almost continuously flowering plants. It is usual when cutting a spike off after it has been in flower for two months or more to find that the flower spike will break again into flower from a side growth. This is not always desirable. If the plant is not strong enough, pinch the second spike out.

These wonderful orchids also have the habit of producing in the case of some species adventitious growths on the flower spikes which may be bent down into the rim of the pot and fixed with a little wire and fresh moss. Phalaenopsis love to be grown in pots with many holes in them or baskets, and are perhaps best suspended from wires, always remembering that they must be kept heavily shaded.

Phalaenopsis flowers are amongst the most beautifully chiselled and beautifully textured flowers in the world. They are known in their country of origin as the 'Moth Orchid', ('El Mariposa'). The shades vary from white to pink (*schilleriana*), but today there are being gradually introduced new hybrids raised from such species as *lueddemanniana,* a yellow form and a purple form; from *cornu-cervi* and *violacea*; and the lovely miniature *rosea*. There are also one or two yellow hybrids through *mannii* and *lueddemanniana* var. *boxalli* and it looks as if the future is going to hold some lovely new creations for us. Recent R.H.S. awards (1969) have proved this.

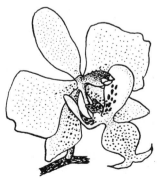

Phalaenopsis schillerana

7

Indoor Culture of Orchids

~~~~~~~~~~~~~~~~~~~~~~~~

IN HER excellent book 100 *Indoor Plants* (Blandford Press), Mrs Muller-Idzerda states correctly: 'It is gradually being realised that it is quite possible to grow orchids in the house, but they are not recommended *often enough* (my italics) so that it is only occasionally that they are seen in a dwelling house'.

I have been asked so many times since *Orchids and Their Cultivation* was first published, to write a few notes on orchids best suited to indoor culture that I am constrained in this present edition to do so.

There is a certain amount of luck in the culture of orchids indoors. With Wardian cases or miniature greenhouses built into the window sills the chances of success are considerable, but I imagine that not more than every other person who attempts to grow orchids without such frames succeeds. The following points are worthy of note:

Those desirous of growing orchids within a dwelling room, or hall, or porch out-number those who wish to grow them under the normal, if almost equally artificial, conditions of a greenhouse.

In the first place we must consider *where,* in what room, or part of the house they are to be grown. Selection of the window (for in all cases it is desirable to grow the plants in close proximity to light), is thus the *first consideration.* Ideally, but not invariably in this country, the room chosen should be centrally heated.

The first and most likely place to choose would in all probability be in front of a window in a sun-warmed living room, facing ideally south or south-west. Such a room in this country is associated with occasional fires, perhaps from 8 a.m. to 11 p.m., and only rarely with full central heating. Themperature will almost surely fluctuate between 45° F. (7° C.) and 75° F. (24° C.). The light at its best (in summer) will probably equal

67

some 2,000 ft candles at 2–3 ft distance from the window and not drop much below 1,000 ft candles at 1 ft distance in the winter. Such a 'window–site' and the orchids that will thrive in it I shall denote by the easy reference 'X', because with it is associated the culture of more or less xerophytic orchids (i.e., sun–loving plants that withstand drought for long periods).

Should the room be centrally heated to say 60° F. (15–16° C.) minimum and 65° F. (18° C.) maximum, it is possible to grow the lovely genus of Cattleyas and the allied hybrids. In countries; like Canada, where the room temperatures are kept as high as 70° F. (21° C.), Phalaenopsis, too, are successfully grown.

The second and equally convenient 'window–site' is the one that faces north (or N.E. or N.W.). It is often associated in towns with an office, a reception room, a dental surgery, or a landing alcove that simply begs for the cheerful presence of a flowering plant. Such a window is ideal for shade–loving plants such as the Paphiopedilum (Slipper Orchid). The temperature here is, even in Britain, more likely to be found constant by reason of some form or other of central heating. It would, I shall assume not vary much more than 20° F. (11° C.) between say 45–65° F. (7–18° C.). It would be permanently shady and even near the glass rarely exceed 800–1,000 ft candles in light intensity. I shall therefore denote this type of 'window–site' and the appropriate orchids by 'N' (north).

The third section into which one might class window-cultures is perhaps the most desirable. This culture involves a Wardian case or miniature greenhouse usually on a table or a suitable stand, which should be placed within the area of a large window with light available from the broadest possible angle. It would face south, but could equally face S.W. or S.E. What it *must* include is a large moisture tray on a table the edge of which is not less than 2 ft (in the winter) and 3 ft (in the summer) from the glass. If the window faced S.E. or S.W. the tray would be ideally 1 ft nearer in each season. (See below). The tray should be a moisture tray in the fullest sense, and it could be slightly heated by a low-tension wire soil-heater. The tray would be made of metal or preferably fibre glass or plastic, and kept filled with breeze or shingle. This in turn would be kept topped up with water, on the whole there being superimposed a Wardian case cover with suitable ventilation. Ventilation should be provided both at the top and the bottom of the case. This third section could include many tropical orchids and would require conditions of central heating and not drop below 60–65° F. (15–18° C.), nor fluctuate unless exceptionally (which would not harm them) more than 5–10° F. (3–5° C.) Orchids in this section are denoted by the letter 'M' for moisture.

If the indoor orchids are not to be grown within a window frame or Wardian case, they should in all circumstances be placed on inverted pots which, in turn, are placed on pans or trays of shingle kept topped up with water. This allows at least a certain amount of moisture to evaporate round the plant. Such plants which are not grown in a frame or case should be taken into the bathroom from time to time and sponged, or even left there during the period of bathing. The moisture and warmth will do the plant good.

LIST OF ORCHIDS ADAPTABLE TO INDOOR CULTURE

X equals xerophytic types. Mostly suited to dry, warm, very sunny rooms, with certain extremes of temperature. 48–78° F. (10–28° C.). These plants still need watering regularly when in growth.

M equals moisture loving types that should have a moisture tray and over-frame (or a fully enclosed Wardian case) with S.E., S. or S.W. aspect, and 60° F. (15–16° C.) minimum.

N equals North-window types that like permanent shade and fairly constant temperatures between 50 and 60° F. (10 and 15° C.).

X

ACCOMMODATION

such as a south-facing morning room, conservatory, verandah, or an upper-floor flat with S.E., S. or S.W. angle window.

Ansellia spp.
Bifrenaria spp.
   (harrisoniae).
Brassavola glauca.
Brassavola perrinii.
*Brassocattleya heatonensis.
*Cattleya hybrids.
Cattleya intermedia.
Cattleya loddigesii.
Cymbidium giganteum.
*Cymbidium tracyanum.

Dendrobium infundibulum.
Dendrobium kingianum.
*Dendrobium nobile and
   hybrids.
Dendrobium pierardii.
Dendrobium parishii.
Dendrobium primulinum.
*Dendrobium jamesianum.
Dendrobium thyrsiflorum.
*Epidendrum aromaticum.
Epidendrum cinnabarinum.
Epidendrum
   atropurpureum.
Ionopsis paniculata.
*Laelia anceps.
*Laelia autumnalis.

*Lycaste cruenta.
Lycaste deppei.
*Lycaste skinneri and others.
Mormodes collosus.
*Odontoglossum
   bictoniense.
*Odontoglossum grande.
Odontoglossum maculatum.
Odontoglossum nebulosum.
Odontoglossum
   schlieperianum.
*Odontoglossum
   uroskinneri.
Oncidium forbesii,
   marshallianum.
*Oncidium incurvum.

Outstandingly Good★

69

*Cymbidium lowianum.
Cymbidium hybrids.
Dendrobium aureum.
*Dendrobium chrysotoxum.

*Laelia gouldiana.
Lissochilus krebsii.
*Lycaste aromatic.
Lycaste candida.

Oncidium papilio.
*Oncidium varicosum.
Oncidium
wentworthianum.

M

ACCOMMODATION
See X. *Almost any living room, given warmth.*

*Aerides odoratum.
*Cattleya skinneri.
Cattleya loddigesii.
Cirrhopetalum
rothschildianum.
Cirrhopetalum Louis
Sander.
Coelogyne mooreana.

Cymbidium eburneum.
Dendrobium dearii.
Dendrobium sanderae.
Huntleya burtii.
*Laelia dayana.
Laelia pumila.
Miltonia vexillaria and
hybrids.
*Paphiopedilum barbatum.
Paphiopedilum bellatulum.
*Paphiopedilum callosum.
Paphiopedilum ciliolare.

*Paphiopedilum concolor.
*Paphiopedilum niveum.
*Paphiopedilum tonsum.
*Phalaenopsis amabilis and
others.
Rhynchostylis coelestis.
Rhynchostylis retusa.
*Vanda coerulescens.
Vanda lamellata.
Vanda hybrids.
Warscewiczella discolor
etc., etc.

N

Suitable for a N. landing or lobby window, a N.E., N., N.W. porch entrance, or any shadowed window with outlook on to an area and reflected light only.

*Masdevallia schroederiana.
*Masdevallia tovarensis.
Maxillaria picta.
Maxillaria rufescens.
Maxillaria sanderiana.
Maxillaria tenuifolia and
others.

*Paphiopedilum insigne
sanderae.
Phragmipedium
longifolium.
Phragmipedium schlimii
and hybrids.
Renanthera imschootiana.
Sobralia macrantha.
Sobralia xantholeuca.
Sophronitis grandiflora and
cernua.
Stenoglottis longifolia.
Vanda amesiana.
Vanda coerulea.
Vanilla planifolia.
Zygopetalum machayii.
etc., etc.

*Coelogyne cristata.
*Epiphronitis veitchii.
Epidendrum O'Brienianum.
Eria convallarioides.
Eria ferruginea.
Eria hyacinthoides.
Eria obesa.
Masdevallia coccinea and
varieties.
Outstandingly Good *

Odontoglossum pulchellum.
Oncidium aurosum.
*Oncidium ornithorynchum.
*Oncidium sphacelatum.
Ornithidium sophronitis.
Paphiopedilum
fairieanum.
Paphiopedilum insigne
hybrids.

Paphiopedilum is restricted to the temperate species.

I feel that what applies to the normal greenhouse culture of orchids should do so equally with an 'indoor' culture. If *you* feel comfortable in a room, so will the plants be happy and thrive therein. Avoid draughts; aridity in summer; over-moist conditions in winter. Do not burn the plants in the sun. Do not try to grow them in cellar-cool and over-shady conditions. Develop your 'feel' for the plants. *Think* about them sometimes.

Select your plants carefully according to the optimum condition you can provide indoors. Let me illustrate this. You have, let us say, the advantage of being retired and free to a great degree, but live in a small cottage with small windows which are tree-shadowed. You love trees, and so you have not the heart to cut that one down. Neither would I. So do not try to grow any orchids. But—there is the airy glass-sided porch entrance at the back! Glazed on both sides, facing south-west, all you have to do is to push the door out, glaze the upper panels, and there you have a miniature greenhouse by the simple erection of four shelves at two levels, two on each side: the south side for sun-loving types, the north side for shade-loving ones.

Again you may be away all day and many weekends, and live in a top-floor flat. But you have a superb large window facing north-east, right over a radiator! How ideal this could be for orchids and many other plants for you will benefit by the early morning sunlight and shade the rest of the day. The plants need thus not be moved daily. A moisture tray, close proximity to the glass, and the slipper orchids, *Coelogyne cristata,* perhaps even a Cymbidium or two will grow and flower well.

Light values. This is a very important factor which does really predetermine whether or not you can even consider growing orchids. Some friend will have a light meter—if you are not yourself keen on photography. Measure your light values in and near certain windows that you favour. 500 up to a 1,000 ft candles (and a little more) could grow the 'N' plants—or some of them anyway. 700 minimum and up to a 1,500 could grow the 'M' list, and 1,000/2,000 the 'X' list. Remember when the sun is behind clouds that 500 ft candles 2 ft from the glass may well equal 700 1 ft nearer. Similarly 1,000 candles 1 ft away may become 2,000 plus when the sun is out.

LIGHT-VALUE DETERMINATION IN FOOTCANDLES

With a normal exposure meter with film-speed indicator set at ASA 100, the speed reading of 1/25 of a second, the f settings that follow will show the equivalent footcandles:

f 1.4	16 footcandles
f 2	32 ,,
f 2.8	64 ,,
f 4	128 ,,
f 5.6	250 ,,
f 8	500 ,,
f 11	1,000 ,,
f 16	2,000 ,,
f 22	4,000 ,,

Setting the exposure meter at ASA 50 or ASA 25 will give illuminations two or four times larger, respectively, than in the above table.

N.B. The light meter must of course be pointed *to* the light.

Never shade in the accepted greenhouse sense. Better to move your plants further away from the glass. This is easily done. A frame on a table can be wheeled or pushed back a foot or two in the sunny hours towards mid-day.

A tray of quite simple construction can slide back on metal brackets lined up with the window-sill. (Sill plus bracket to equal 3 ft). If the tray is 2 ft deep there results a most useful movement of 12–18 in. to and from the glass—18 in. if the tray is drawn into the room over the brackets with a 6 in. overlap.

Avoid draughts like poison. Bad for human beings who can at least dose themselves when they 'catch cold', they are worse for a plant. The unfortunate chilled plant may lose all its leaves and must wait perhaps a full year to put on a new set of growths if thus checked. Take a lot of trouble to avoid a draughty corner or window. An open window will do much less harm—indeed often good, for example on a warm wet rainy August day—than ten minutes cutting draught on a winter day.

Moisture trays, either on the window-sill or within a Wardian case (this is the equivalent of a miniature greenhouse) are essential really if you have more than one or two orchids or other plants. With an odd plant it would suffice to place the pot within a larger pot or container, filling the intervening space with stone chippings, coke dust, moss, and even sand, or a combination of all or some of these moisture retaining media. The double pot can then be stood on a deep (1 in.) saucer, and *in the growing season* (usually spring and summer) this saucer can be topped up with soft water (rain if possible). If not tap water will do, unless it is excessively chlorinated which you can soon *see*.

A tray can be a simple baker's tray, or an attractive copper receptacle, or simply a zinc affair painted to match the window-sill, and should if possible be 2 in. deep. It must be filled with fine gravel and/or sand, or coke breeze, or granite chippings, or anything you fancy that is receptive to moisture. Only 1 in. of this depth (maximum) should be filled up with water. Never *top up* with water. There are many reasons for this, but especially to assist evaporation of water around the plant, and ventilation of the air immediately above the tray, and ensure adequate drainage of the plants staged on it.

Feeding. A little may be indulged in. Let the plant seek the food. Never water it indiscriminately. Rather let the plant suck it up from beneath. *One drop* of Liquinure per tea-cup of water is ample, and only to be used in the spring and summer. There are other suitable manures. Chose a real and natural one. Avoid chemical fertilisers, and of course all those excessively advertised.

Watering can be done with a tea cup too! My guess—and it *is* a guess, for your plant alone can tell you—is one cup per week for 'N' plants in 5–5½ in. pot for example, and two per week for 'X' plants of the same sized pot, and perhaps only one per 10 days for similar 'M' plants in a Wardian case. This for summer months. In the winter half this amount would probably be too much for the 'X' plants that are at rest, and certainly it would suffice for the 'N's'.

If you supplemented central heating at a steady 70° F. (21° C.) with a 1 kw. electric fire in a living room 15 × 15 ft the 'cup-per-week' in the summer advice would be sadly out and might well need to be a tea-pot per week! Better however, to err on the dry side than leave a plant sodden for weeks and months on end.

Spraying. A little very fine atomiser will not harm most plants, but the tendency is to soak them, and so *unless* you have what almost equals a scent spray for lightness of density avoid spraying, but rather wash your plant with a sponge occasionally. Yes, in the bath! Bi-monthly I would say if you have the time.

Never spray flowers. Spray the *under* surfaces of the leaves rather than the upper.

When buying orchids, or selecting types from a list bear in mind *firstly* the available shade-light values, then the vigour of the plant, and thirdly floriferousness.

Light loving orchids such as Laelias, *Vanda amesiana, Odontoglossum grande* for the south window; Slipper Orchids mostly for the shady corners near south windows, or the full light of a north window, as also *Coelogyne cristata* or Masdevallias for example; but the irresistible *Aerides quinquenervis* you may have bought at a flower show in a weak moment, you *must* house in a moist frame or Wardian case in optimum conditions.

Never buy a weakly plant. They are often available at much reduced prices and are ideal for a 'quick collector' who has (*a*) a greenhouse and (*b*) an aptitude already acquired for growing orchids. Not for those limited to growing within four walls, are such bargains. Choose rather fewer mature, *flowered* plants for a given sum. *Paphiopedilum insigne* of *circa* 10–12 growths to give 2–4 flowers and a really fine large plant of *Cymbidium lowianum,* which should have at least 5–6 bulbs for the outlay, and be inspike (carry a flower spike), will obviously cost you less than a modern hybrid.

Since most orchids flower but once a year—albeit often, as with Paphiopedilums and Cymbidiums for six to eight weeks on end—buy if you can a *flowered* plant. Some plants are blind. Small plants will often take years to flower. Your plant should be at least six years old, which usually means it has 5–6 good bulbs or leafed growths.

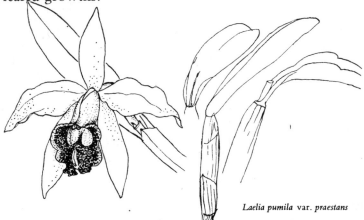

Laelia pumila var. *praestans*

Miniatures. I cannot end this chapter without a strong recommendation to those who live in towns in small rooms to consider the many delightful *miniature* orchids! They can be grown in a cactus house of a couple or so cubic feet, or in a 'barn-cloche' frame costing a few *shillings*! Some are lovely. I list a few on page 73. All are *gems*. All love moisture. None grow much over 6 in. high.

Other 'gems' to grow and once known as the 'Jewel' orchids are the foliage orchids grown for the sheer beauty of their leaves, of which the best known genera are Anoectochilus and Goodyearas (from the Himalayas to Korea), Haemaria (Malayan Peninsula) and Macodes (Java to New Guinea) as also the delicate *Dossinia marmorata* from Sarawak. Alas these are all rare! If you acquire them grow them in *heavy* shade, a warm as you can, preferably under a bell-jar, or old clock-glass, with a wedge under one side for ventilation. My favourite is *Anoectochilus setaceus,* but almost as lovely are *A. dawsonianus* and *roxburghii, Macodes petola* and *Haemaria discolor.* The veins in their leaves often literally run gold! Pleione is another very popular genus.

A SELECTION OF MINIATURE ORCHIDS
(those that rarely exceed 6 in. in vertical height)

Aerides japonicum.
Angraecum distichum.
Anoectochilus—all spp.

Brassavola glauca.
Brassia elegantula.
Bulbophyllum—most spp.

Cattleya acklandiae
Cattleya aclaniae.
Cattleya dolosa.
Cattleya forbesii.
Cattleya luteola.
Cirrhopetalum—all spp.
Coelogyne cristata.
Coelogyne miniata.
Coelogyne pulchella.
Coelogyne rossiana.
Coelogyne sanderae.
Cymbidium pumilum.
Cymbidium tigrinum.

Dendrobium—many spp. are dwarf such as aureum, capillipes, coelogyne, cymbidioides, linguiforme, loddigesii, senile, etc.

Earina suaveolens.
Epidendrum and Eria, many of which are dwarf, such as Epid. polybulbon and Eria globulifera.

Laelic jongheana.
Laelia pumila and vars.

Masdevallia—most of the spp.
Maxillarias—many spp. including picta.

Odontoglossum—several spp. such as cervantesii, krameri, naevium, oerstedii, rossii.
Oncidium—many spp. such as bicolor, cheirophorum, concolor, iridifolium, longipes, olivaceum, pulchellum, pumilum, triquetrum, etc.

Paphiopedilum—many of the spp. are suitable such as niveum, concolor, bella-tulum, etc.

Phalaenopsis cornu-cervi.
Phalaenopsis mannii.
Phalaenopsis parishii.
Platyclinis (syn. Dendro-chilium filiformis.
Pleiones—all spp.
Pleurothallis—many spp.
Polystachya luteola.
Polystachya pubescens.

Restrepia—all spp.

Saccolabium acutifolium.
Saccolabium ampullaceum.
Saccolabium bellinum.
Sophronitis grandiflora.

Trichopilia suavis.
Trichopilia tortilis.

Vanda alpina.
Vanda amesiana.
Vanda pumila.

Zygopetalum stapelioides.
Zygopetalum xanthinum.

8

The Culture of Hardy Orchids in the Garden

I REGRET to have to admit that I have only met with a modicum of success in the culture of hardy orchids. It is a technique all on its own, and I feel that I cannot do better than to call on a man who in the not so distant past successfully grew many varieties of hardy orchids out of doors. I refer to Fred Streeter who will be known to most of you. There follows an article by him which he has specially written at my request on the subject of hardy orchids and their culture.

HARDY ORCHIDS

It is not generally known that orchids can be grown outside on north borders or in frames in the British Isles. They come chiefly from North America, but there are many European species as well. They are perfectly easy to grow once you give them as near their natural conditions as possible.

Let us take the Cypripediums first, varieties like *spectabile, pubescens* and *acaule,* etc. Take out the existing soil 2 ft deep, no matter what the soil is like. Place a bottom layer of old bricks over the whole bed. Then fill it with two–year–old sifted beech leaves. (Not horse chestnut.) Firm it well down before placing the crowns 12 in. apart on top with the roots well spread out and in lines. Then cover with the leaves to 4 in., leaving the whole nice and level. In very severe weather place a little old bracken over to keep off severe frost, but take it off once the frost has gone. A few degrees of frost will not hurt. The ideal site being on a north border, there should be plenty of moisture except in a very dry season. When they are in full growth before flowering a few real good soakings with rain water will help them. As soon as the buds begin to show place a skeleton frame and tiffany blind over the whole bed to keep off any dews and rain, or the sun if it reaches the bed round four o'clock in the afternoon. This keeps the flowers clean and brings out the colouring. It is a good plan to plant a row of low growing, variegated aubretia round the outside of the bed as this is much smaller than other aubretias. Should there be any slugs or snails you will find them under the neat little cushion of growths where they are easy to find and destroy.

The finest batch I have ever seen was in one of the gardens I served in with 2,000 blooms open at once. It was really magnificent, and visitors from their native home used to say they had not even seen the like in their North American home. (This was Straffan House, Co. Kildare.)

The European species require different treatment. They are best grown on the billiard table or raised bed system, built up some 3 ft or more with either stones or, easier, old railway sleepers. This is a really wonderful garden for elderly people who are unable to stoop much. Put in a treble layer of old bricks and on this a double layer of turves grass–side downwards. Then fill up with a compost made up of rather heavy chopped up loam mixed with peat or sifted beech leaves and limestone chippings, and planted with low growing alpines, with the orchids planted in groups amongst them. This gives them good protection.

Our most successful attempt at growing the European species was in an orchard on a very heavy Sussex clay on which the old compost from the garden formed the mounds for the fruit trees to root into. The orchids were planted on the mounds with great success, many of them with 2 ft long stems, and used for tea table decoration where they were greatly admired.

As a boy at school, I used to hunt for them growing on the chalk on the North Downs at Reigate where at the foot of the hills amongst the trees and undergrowth they did exceedingly well. Then in later years on the South Downs under the beech on the north side I found them much more plentiful, which interested me greatly and which was the cause of the planting in the orchard and lower ground.

Another method of growing is in small pans in a cold house, about twelve bulbs to a pan, like growing crocus species, covering the surface with limestone chippings. Here the great thing is to rest them properly after they have died down. Always water with rain water if possible and from the start of the growing season keep them moist, but never too wet. There are enough natives to make a nice collection. The following were some of the species grown in this manner:

Orchis foliosa, a very handsome plant, really one of the best I think with its long sprays of rosy pink flowers in May and June, and of great interest in any garden. It does well in the boggy part of the rock garden.

The Marsh Orchid, *O. latifolia,* is another beauty with long spikes of purple flowers. This variety also loves a boggy position and is also lovely in June or early summer. There are several varieties with 18-in. stems. One from the Channel Islands called *laxiflora* is well worth a place. It has rich purplish red flowers and is always at home on the rock garden. Good groups of this variety attract attention wherever it is seen. The best known variety is of course *O. maculata.* This requires a richer compost, a nice rich medium loam, peat, flaky leaf soil and three-sixteenths grit, although I have seen it do well in a rich garden soil, and in its wild state in the woods. There are many forms of this variety of which I think *superba* is the best.

Anyone owning a cool or cold greenhouse, similar to the alpine house, can grow these European species in small pans. Give them a rich soil over well drained pans and place the bulbs about 2 in. deep and five to a 5-in. pan. Cover the surface with limestone chippings, and be very careful in the spring when weeds often start before the orchids. I have always found it best to clip these weeds over, rather than pulling them out, and more natural.

Now I am certain anyone interested in these lovely, uncommon plants will find them extremely intriguing. The unfortunate thing about these species growing wild is that they are so often pulled clean out of the ground by people walking through woods being amazed at seeing such beautiful plants growing wild. This pulling up of the stems is the main cause of their becoming scarcer every year.

†FRED STREETER, A.H.R.H.S., V.M.H.

There are, in Britain, one or two outstanding collections of truly hardy orchids. Of easy access to the public I would mention Cambridge Botanic Gardens, and of course Kew Gardens. At Inverleith, Edinburgh, they have (amongst several interesting species), the finest clump of *Orchis maderensis* I have ever seen. Now that rightly or wrongly myxomatosis has reduced our rabbit population to near nil in many countries, there will undoubtedly be a resurgence of our rarer native species to which many will look forward. But the finest single collection south of the border and privately owned since Mr Clarence Eliot's days was undoubtedly that of Mr J. Strangman, Q.C., an incredibly keen amateur who has travelled Europe and the Mediterranean to fill his garden and alpine house with several thousand plants including the following fine hardy orchids:

I *Serapis cordigera, neglecta* and *longipetala,* three fine 'Tongue' orchids.
II 'Bog' orchids such as *Orchis foliosa, sesquipedalis* (a truly magnificent border plant), *latifolia, laxiflora* and *palustris.*
III *Orchis morio, picta, mascula, papilionacea, provincialis* and *pauciflora.*
IV *Orchis sambucina,* both red and yellow forms, and *pallens,* three fine 'Mountain' orchids.
V Of the 'Military' group *Orchis purpurea, simia, militaris* and *longicruris.*
VI Incredibly lovely *Ophrys* (I have seen one form 'Atlantica' with nineteen flowers) such as *fusca, lutea, speculum* and *bombylifora, aranifera, apifera, fuciflora, scolopax, tenthredinifera,* and many fine Italian forms.

The tragedy is that this collection is no longer to be seen and few are available commercially, due to part to the lack of knowledge concerning their germination under glass, in part to their long period of maturescence (eleven years) but in greater part to lack of initiative and capital in horticulture.

I hope that one day all this will be remedied, and you will buy hardy orchids as you would herbaceous plants.

Only comparatively minor use can be made of orchids in England. In the warmer parts, and in certain localities of Ireland and Scotland the true Cypripediums, Bletilla, Calopogons, Calypso and some of the Ophrys and Orchis can be used to advantage, particularly in rock and bog gardens. In one or two specially favourable spots, where the probability of frost is remote, Cymbidiums and *Paphiopedilum insigne* can be used, but such places are the exception with our variable and humid, heavy, atmosphere.

Abroad, the case is quite different. Many Eastern orchids may be grown in the West Indies, and vice versa, e.g., *Phaius grandifolius* has been acclimatised in the West Indies, and in places has become a popular garden plant, flowering and reproducing itself freely, while in Madeira Sobralias grow to perfection out of doors.

So far, however, a very insufficient use has been made of such plants, but it is to be hoped that, in the future, residents in warmer countries will endeavour to enrich their gardens by the use of adaptable orchids from other parts of the globe. Our correspondent, the late Mr Eugene André, writing from Trinidad, said: 'Even where no other orchids are kept, *Vanda teres* and *Vanda* Agnes Joaquim can be grown as garden plants, stuck in shrubs and hedges, or on the top of arbours. They are of great use for cut flowers. Some species of *Vanda teres* sent years ago to H. Nehrling, of Florida, have done quite well in the open.' In Singapore I have seen hedges of terete Vandas.

In Madeira, California and in Sydney, Cymbidiums grow and flower well in the open, and no doubt other orchids would readily adapt themselves—*Vanda coerulea,* the Mexican species, and probably the cooler growing Dendrobiums.

To naturalise orchids, some idea of the climate and conditions in their own habitat is perhaps necessary, but more certain success can be obtained by experimenting with one or two plants, watching as to which grow the better, and then obtaining plants which have been successfully cultivated with them under glass. In Florida enormous efforts have been made by many enthusiastic Americans, both lady and gentleman amateurs, to acclimatise a whole gamut of species and with *great* success.

If well-defined seasons occur where it is desired to naturalise orchids, the limits of such seasons should be stated. As far as possible plants should be procured which grow and flower in somewhat similar seasons.

In Ceylon the weather conditions vary in different parts, and, apart from orchids peculiar to the island, varieties of Dendrobium, Vanda, etc., are found there. Where native species exist, it should be easy with a little care to grow the finer species. Possibly in the cooler districts Maxillarias, Cymbidiums,

Oncidiums, etc., and some Odontoglossums could be adapted.

Odontoglossum crispum and similar orchids which grow under peculiar local conditions should only be attempted in the open air, where such conditions are fairly well represented, or can be more or less closely imitated by natural shelters. Probably in many mountainous countries there are localities where the atmosphere, elevation, etc., are quite in agreement with those of the *crispum* country.

Considerable progress is being made in the culture of orchids in many parts of the world. Given the required temperature, certain orchids can be grown as garden plants, while others require but little artificial protection and certainly far less attention than is given them under glass in England.

In conclusion, I sincerely hope that these notes and brief outlines will be helpful to all readers. I much regret that definite rules on every point cannot be given, but such rules would in many cases be manifestly misleading. Conditions in the south, north, east and west of England are never identical. In fact, it may be said that no localities, however near each other, and no two houses are exactly the same; consequently slight differences have to be made in the management of the shading, airing,

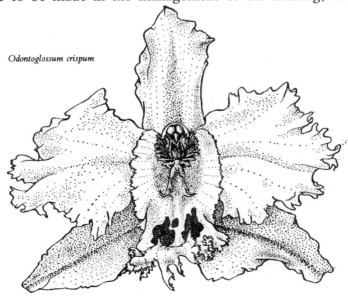

Odontoglossum crispum

watering, etc. Differences which can only be found by observation, and adjusted by common-sense rulings.

On any special difficulties which may arise, I shall be glad to give such advice as I am ablt to. Orchids are so polymorphic and have so adapted themselves to withstand extremes that there is probably not a glasshouse, from which frost is excluded, in which twenty or more different kinds of orchids cannot be easily grown. Moreover, they should give better results, with lower cost and less care, than many other plants commonly grown.

9

Fertilisers and Feeding

ONLY IN recent years has orchid feeding become a serious study. Until the late war it was generally agreed that faint applications of natural manure *around* the plants and the addition of a very small amount of bonemeal, Thompson's fertiliser, Clay's or blood in powered from to terrestrial composts (about an ounce to a bushel) were more than sufficient. Personally I feel it is, and to do more is cheating! Half the fun lies in *growing* a plant as near naturally as possible, but this statement is, I fully realise, based on little real knowledge of what actually happens to a plant in its natural environment, and what the real values of decayed matter around it consist of, I am therefore tempted to risk a little speculation based on experiences of several friends and growers.

Firstly the natural manures. These can best be applied to the grosser rooting and feeding orchids, usually termed terrestrials, and which in cultivation benefit by loam and peat and leaf composts. Undoubtedly fish manure ranks high in value, but as with the above mentioned powdered feeds, only experience can determine the safe *maximum*. In the case of Liquinure which is known to be effective I suggest a teaspoonful to a large pail of water is more than enough. With such liquid forms of manure do not water it in. Let the plant seek it from under. Pour it into a saucer or a baking tin, and only periodically during the growing season place the plant pot in it, up to say 1 in. depth for a few hours. I suggest one week's feeding in three is ample. This and other manures certainly increase the size of the bulbs and flowers, but whether the colour of the flowers is reduced is a moot point. Never burst your bulbs and sheaths by excessive dosing. The plant will surely then collapse—or become virused.

Epiphytes are quite another proposition as are also baby seedlings. A well-balanced (A–Z) nutrient solution can do wonders with these tree loving orchids. Cattleyas and Vandas and Phalaenopsis benefit specially. What better than a nutrient solution without the agar? (see page 101 and 102). You may slightly increase the trace elements at will—even double them. It is an experiment worth trying out, but you will find it hard to prove it worth while, for *perfect* specimens have and are grown with *no* added solution whatsoever.

The great point to make is that you *cannot* feed an orchid without giving it more light. Photosynthesis is in fact just that relationship between light and the capacity of the plant to absorb food which the light playing on the leaf cells enables them to turn into tissue.

Please bear in mind that the following notes are written on the assumption that the reader is growing orchids in England in the usual English composts which are based on pine bark. The American system of growing plants, which is now copied to a great extent on the Continent, usually involves all sorts of unusual materials, not excluding coconut husks, rock chippings and a great variety of other substances which are more or less neutral, but to which the roots will cling *provided* the plants are watered regularly with a 'feed'. This type of feeding I know little about and will not attempt to describe or recommend it. There are many articles to be read in the American Orchid Society's Bulletins which give all sorts of 'feeds' based on substances as far apart as fish emulsion and inorganic materials.

With Epiphytes the feeding must be on a very light scale. They only need a little 'fillip' to boost this meagre pine bark diet. Feed your Epiphytes if you will but only when they are growing freely—in the U.K. usually from February to July or August.

A standard solution is Dr Hoagland's. Make it up as follows: get four pint bottles. In each bottle in turn tip level teaspoons full of (1) potassium acid phosphate, (2) potassium nitrate, (3) calcium nitrate, and (4) magnesium sulphate. Top the bottles up with rainwater or tap water if the supply is soft. These stock bottles are then used for feeding as follows. Pour one tablespoonful of potassium acid phosphate to two of magnesium sulphate to five each of potassium and calcium nitrate into a gallon watering can of clean rain water and add with a pipette ten to twelve drops of phosphoric acid.

One of the oldest formulas and simplest was used at the turn of the century by the late father of a grand and truly amateur orchid grower, Mr Clive Cookson of Hexham, and consisted simply of two fertilisers in common use. Three ounces of potassium nitrate and two of ammonium phosphate were tipped into a large jar or bottle and topped up with the lovely soft waters from the Cumberland Moors. A quarter of a pint of this stock solution was diluted into a 5 gallons of water for feeding purposes.

One of my friends, a very keen and successful amateur grower, uses Liquinure to a very great extent. He even puts one or two drops in a glass phial with a rubber end and pushes the roots of his Vandas into these phials. They suck up the Liquinure at a tremendous rate and literally grow as you watch them—in fact as much as an inch in a week. I did not in this case notice that the flowering was in any way improved. What I did notice was that there was a tendency for the whole greenhouse staging, flooring and woodwork to be covered with green slime. This, I think, is most unpleasant and not necessary.

At my nursery at Selsfield we use literally only five manures. Two of them are used with Cymbidiums and one or two of the rather lush growing, heavy feeding plants such as Zygopetalums. To these we give hoof and horn and/or bonemeal in large chips above the crocks, or in granulated form mixed with the compost. (One 2 in. potful to a bushel.)

The other two manures we use are very excellent ones. The first is a liquid seaweed which is sprayed on to the plants during the growing months. What we actually use is Maxicrop. It is easily diluted and gives off a rather pleasant seaweedy smell. It is impossible to overdo this spray 'feed' for the plants will only absorb through their leaves what they want. The other feeds we very occasionally use are Bio No. 5 and Sprayfer. This is a soapy mixture and softens the water nicely, and I like to add it from time to time at my own discretion, but rarely more than once a month, in the spring and summer to the main water supply. This supply is, of course, rain water. These spray 'feeders' are of great value for the epiphytes, and in particular for the Vandas and Phalaenopsis.

The finest and most successful manure that I have ever seen used is urine. In the Far East this is most extensively used with vandaecious orchids. It must of course be heavily diluted if used in this country in greenhouses. (Liquinure is the nearest equivalent.)

MANURES

There has been, and still is, considerable controversy on the subject of using fertilisers in the cultivation of orchids. We strongly deprecate direct application to all epiphytal orchids and to many terrestrial orchids, particularly the smaller-growing species, except, of course, where hydroponic culture obtains.

Judiciously used, i.e., when the plants are in full growth and root action, Phaius, Cymbidium and green-leaved Paphiopedilums which have not been potted in the current year, are benefited by a weak solution of manure obtained from a bushel of soot to 3 bushels of cow manure, placed in bags in a tub of rainwater, used diluted to the colour of weak tea, and given to the plants occasionally (about once a week in the growing season).

Calanthes may be treated far more liberally and solutions of sheep and horse manure given them, the strength being increased as the plants attain full vigour. Even artificial manures are applied by some gardeners with benefit, but unless, with exception as the Calanthes, very carefully and thoughtfully used, all manures are dangerous when applied directly to the roots.

The more natural, and therefore better, method is to damp the floors of the houses with the cow and soot liquid in the evenings, when all danger from the sun is past. A mild odour is given off, and the foliage of all orchids benefits, assuming a darker green, healthier hue. The fumes are entirely gone by morning and the operation may be repeated every evening during the growing season—say from April to the end of September.

An old-fashioned practice was to scatter soot and lime mixed, on the floors, etc., in the evening; but the drawback is that the lime generates the ammonia from the soot, particularly if the latter is new and raw, too quickly, and the fumes produced in a spasm are too fierce, and often damage the foliage. If the soot and lime be thrown down, they should be used in such small quantities that the eyes and throat of anyone entering the house directly after its use are not affected. On the whole it is much better, particularly for amateurs, either to avoid the use of manures entirely, or to confine themselves to the use of weak liquid manures on the floor. If natural manures are not available, then liquid solutions can be made of guano, or other manures.

Attempts have been made to obtain medical formulæ which

should help the orchids, but the results have not been satisfactory. The benefits obtained have proved to be very temporary in their nature, and when deprived of the stimulant the plants invariably deteriorate. Like those given natural manures at the roots, they seem to be far more susceptible to diseases, changes of temperature, and insects.

We must admit, however, that from what correspondents from abroad tell us, manure, chiefly cow, is freely used on orchids which with them grow in the open air. Dendrobiums, Vandas, etc., are heavily manured and apparently respond freely to its use; growths and vigour resulting in many instances beyond that which can be obtained here, due to great sunlight, in which they grow under natural conditions.

Such plants, however, probably remain under the same conditions for long periods, and are in many cases grown out of doors.

Manure, in small enough quantities, can be used experimentally and successfully with other orchids including Miltonias and Cymbidiums, but immediately after an overdose is given, virus ensues. Thus, we repeat, for safety follow the above instructions.

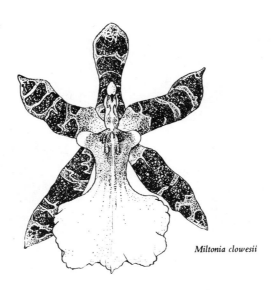

Miltonia clowesii

CARBON DIOXIDE FEEDING

The burning of propane gas to produce CO_2 (carbon dioxide) is undoubtedly of enormous advantage during the light hours of the day and has a tremendous affect on the growth of the plants and their flowering. The trouble is it is very expensive commercially and not inexpensive from the amateur's point of view. The picture on page 150 of an amateur's greenhouse which is fully automatic and fed by CO_2 for six to eight hours a day according to the light values is a proof of the enormous success that carbon dioxide can be made to add to the culture of Orchids.

10

Pests

ANTS ARE a serious pest in as much as they carry and spread many aphids and scales which they appear to 'milch'. Keep them *down*. We find that liberal dusting with insecticide every three months keeps them away, although I believe it does not actually kill them. Although it does prove a wonderful preventative measure. For an amateur, however, with a small collection I think it is simpler to spray the plants or dust them if more convenient.

It might be expected, from the polymorphic nature of the order and the many countries and localities from which they are collected, that orchids would be liable to many diseases and strange insect pests. Such, however, is not the case. There are a few—a very few—insects peculiar to some genera but on the whole orchids under cultivation are less subject to insect attacks than are other plants.

Thrips, aphis, red spider and several species of scale (coccus) insect are among the more common. Perhaps the worst and most common pest is the thrips, a very small, elongated, extremely mobile and almost invisible creature of grey to brown hues, some $1/12$ in. long.

Thrips are particularly fond of the young growths of Odontoglossums, Paphiopedilum, Miltonias, and apparently all flowers, in which they find both shelter and food. Attacks are the more prevalent in the early spring and summer, but no season is really free from them. They delight in dry heat and, unless checked, breed rapidly at all seasons. The insects are so minute that often their presence is not suspected until the effects are seen in contorted flower-buds, disfigured flowers and growths. Their presence is usually first noticed by glaucous patches on the leaves, especially the young growths, at nodal points. Like the red spider, the thrips thrive in dry hot atmospheres, and usually hies from the nearest hedge. Usually the first indications can be seen on the young growths of Oncidiums, Odontoglossums and similar growing plants, when, by holding a plant up to the light, small circular semi-transparent spots can be noticed.

In Paphiopedilums, particularly the mottled leaved kinds, a rusty patch is in evidence on either surface of the leaves. On flowers, it is usually the edges of the segments, where they overlap, which show rusty, whitish and often blackish discoloration.

Such evidences are the effect of thrips and, as prevention is better than cure, every effort should be made to detect these and all other insects as soon as possible, before they obtain a hold and give too evident proof of their existence. An occasional dusting, spray or dipping in an insecticide solution, is recommended as a preventative. Used as a cure, the treatment should be repeated at least twice at 3-week intervals.

Should there be a heavy infestation of thrips in the greenhouse it is perhaps advisable to use one of the more modern preparations but allow for the fact that its effect will wear off, and then repeat as a preventative at regular intervals of, say, two months. Malathion is also an excellent killer of red spider with which insect the next paragraph deals.

Red Spider of vivid coral hue, slowly mobile, about the size of a pinhead seldom attacks orchids as seriously as do thrips; but it will attack all orchids, given favourable conditions. Its presence may be detected by leprous white patches on the foliage. The arid atmosphere in which red spider revels is antipodal to that which the orchid loves, hence where the orchid luxuriates, red spider seldom obtains a hold. Remember with these red spiders that there are often many thousands of little eggs invisible to the eye, which will develop into spiders and must also be dealt with. Therefore, an application of insecticide should be repeated within ten days.

Scale insects. Numerous forms attack orcids both under cultivation and in their own homes. They are often present on imported orchids, particularly Brazilian species, which should always be examined on arrival for these and other insects. Such infected plants should be brushed with methylated spirit before being placed in the greenhouse. Mealy scale unfortunately gets right into the compost and under the rhizomes, and must be removed by a toothbrush or other brush that will penetrate below the rhizomes.

Cattleyas and allied plants are peculiarly liable to injury from scale, as the insects find hiding-places beneath the membranous sheaths. For a small collection, the old-fashioned remedy, sponging and brushing with soft soap and water, is effective. If scale be suspected underneath the sheaths, the old membranous sheaths must be stripped from the Cattleyas. The rhizomes must be carefully examined and cleaned with a tooth brush. When insects are not present nor suspected, the membranes should never be stripped off. They are nature's protection against extremes of heat and cold. A painter's small sash brush is useful for cleaning the leaf axils in such sheathing-leaved plants as Ærides, Vandas, Cymbidiums, etc. At least one of the scale family known as *Parlatoria Pseudo-Aspidiotus* is very persistent and pernicious, in as much as it propagates very fast and appears on superficial inspection to be dead after dipping. Under the apparently dried dead scale will be found, on turning it over carefully, a whole family of live creamy-white young (from 10 to 20). They do enormous damage by sapping the leaf juices. In six months a large house can be infected from end to end. If time is not too short sponge or brush each leaf.

Use a really potent insecticide if the outbreak is severe, dipping each affected plant thoroughly, and three weeks later spraying thoroughly the same plants, which should be kept together and apart from the clean plants. Do *not* use Malathion, or any similar phosphorous preparation without making yourself fully aware of the real dangers. Undiluted, one drop can be fatal. Read the directions. Wear protective clothing. Keep a pail of water and soap handy to wash any skin that might get affected by a splash. Dip the plants at ground level. When spraying walk and work in a backwards direction.

The great thing to remember with all these insecticides is that they change in popularity. Seek advice from a commercial grower before choosing the latest best 'killer'.

Lycastes, Zygopetalums, Phaius and similar broad-leaved orchids are liable to a species of scale often confused with mealy bug, due to the insect covering its eggs with a mealy substance.

The most effective remedy is brushing with methylated spirits, taking care that the eggs are not distributed to other parts of the house or plants.

Ants, though not injurious to orchids, do an immense amount of harm by carrying scale from one plant to another, placing them in awkward positions and endeavouring to conceal them by covering them with small pieces of compost. Probably no insect is harder to destroy. They escape fumigants and sprays, and usually make their nests in an inaccessible place. Their numbers used to be diminished by traps such as small bottles containing a little linseed or olive oil. Fresh putty attracts them and numbers may be killed by re-rolling the putty as soon as covered by ants. Bones, bacon rinds, etc., may be laid down and the ants if attracted can be destroyed. Salt and boracic powder may be placed in odd corners, provided that when dissolved they cannot contaminate the water used for watering plants. Search should be made for the ants' nests, and these destroyed.

Woodlice or slaters do considerable damage to small plants and the tips of roots. Boracic powder may be scattered in their haunts, but the most effective remedies are traps. Potatoes cut in halves and slightly hollowed, with a nick cut in them to allow ingress to these pests, may be laid on the stages and examined each day. Pots partially filled with hay answer the same purpose, as do flat pieces of wood laid on the ground, but the better method is prevention by cleanliness and absence of any rubbish under the stagings, etc., which serve as hiding-places for them. Derris dust is a most useful deterrent.

Cockroaches and crickets are very fond of Cattleya flowers, particularly albinos. They may be hunted at night, trapped by means of sweetened beer placed in the bottom of glass jars, or poisoned by any of the advertised beetle pastes. As with woodlice cleanliness is the best deterrent to cockroaches which prefer dry, warm places near hot-water pipes in which to shelter, while the slugs and snails like cool and damp, but not wet corners.

Mealy bug is very infrequent on orchids. Rodriguezias are probably more susceptible to this pest than are other orchids.

Vandas, and heavily bracted Guatemalan and Mexican species must be closely watched for this pest, more commonly associated with plants other than orchids that are introduced into the greenhouses.

Greenfly may occasionally be noticed, but is easily exterminated by light fumigations or sprayings. Keep a sharp lookout during show time in the spring for greenfly on buds and flowers. It is then in particular that they come in from the outside hedges and cause a nasty, disfiguring, black, sticky, substance to ruin the buds and flowers. It may, however, be washed off if caught in time.

Cattleya fly (*Isosoma orchidearum*). This pest, probably the most insidious of all the insects which attack orchids, appears to have been imported with *Cattleya labiata*. This serious pest is practically never seen today in England. Apart from the system of certification of imported and exported plants, a nurseryman would never risk keeping a plant on his nursery which showed signs of this fly. Allied genera are liable to be attacked. The mature insect is a small, blackish fly, ⅛ in. in length, but the mischief is caused by its larvæ. Eggs are deposited in the plant and the larvæ find a congenial hiding-place and food in the centre of the growth, causing premature activity and an apparently vigorous growth, the interior of which is eventually eaten to some extent; stunted, abortive pseudo-bulbs are the result, on which may be seen the holes through which the insects have escaped. Imported Cattleyas should be carefully scrutinised and, if the larva's presence is suspected, left for eight hours thoroughly immersed in tepid water. Should premature growths appear swollen at the base and abnormally pointed, cut them off and burn them. If small, round holes in the new growths suggest that the insects have matured, frequent fumigations should be resorted to.

Root fly. An insect with similar habits to *Isosoma* frequently attacks Cattleya roots and forms a swelling just below the root tip. Only those roots on the surface of, or outside, the compost are, as a rule, attacked. Unless in great numbers but little harm results, as the absorbent portion of the roots gain increased size. The effective remedy is cutting off the infected portions and burning them.

Boring insects. Imported Dendrobiums are sometimes infected by boring beetles. The species most prevalent, but fortunately infrequently met with, is *Xyleborous perforans*. Effects of its ravages are easily seen in imported plants and, when suspected, portions of the pseudo-bulbs may be cut off.

The great secret is to vary the spraying programme as insects tend to become immune from any one insecticide. Malathesco-60 is of great value and popular today, but must be used with great care (macs, rubber gloves, and sou'westers). If attention is paid to the admission of air and to occasional fumigations or spraying with some deterrent compound serious outbreaks can be avoided.

Spraying with insecticides should always be carried out rather late in the day, but with pipes sufficiently warm to dry up any excessive moisture before night in dull weather. In spraying, if possible use an automatic sprayer as by its use more even distribution can be gained than by a syringe.

Springtails. Best controlled by dipping the infected base of the pot in almost any insecticide solution. This solution should also be sprayed on top of the inverted pots should the plants be standing on inverted pots.

Slugs. Slugs and snails are best killed by a metaldehyde mixture, or kept in check by night-killing sorties when 'torch and heel' are used. Flower spikes may be protected by cotton wool, over which no slug will crawl.

Spotting. This is caused by excessive moisture relative to temperature. The remedy lies in increasing ventilation when possible, or alternatively reducing relative humidity.

Damping Off. Frequently leaves and/or bulbs are found to rot. This is usually caused by bruising, or perforation by insects. If noticed in the initial stages the remedy is to scrape away the rotted portion then *lime* or *sulphur* heavily. If the rot in bulb or leaf is only noticed in an advanced stage, cut the whole bulb cleanly off as near the rhizome as possible with a sharp knife dipped in alcohol. Lime the cut.

Phalaenopsis and one or two other orchids are susceptible to a strange type of rotting. This begins with a spot on the leaf which eventually holes and spreads outwardly. There is a wonderful cure for this and other diseases connected with the rotting or damping off of the leaves. It is an American product known as Orthocide popularly old under the name of Captan, 50 per cent wettable. This powder is obtainable in England under the trade name Thiram. We use it a lot on our nursery and it is most effective.

All the pests mentioned in the foregoing pages can be successfully controlled with modern insecticides. Any garden centre or garden supply shop will stock a wide range to choose from. If in doubt consult an expert or use an alternative insecticide. Insecticides have not been recommended by name, as these are continually changing in the shops. New solutions are always replacing old ones which have been withdrawn or banned by the authorities. Whatever insecticide is used, it is important to remember that these are highly concentrated and are deadly poisons. They should be stored carefully, and kept well out of reach of children, as well as far away from fish ponds. When in use, one should always wear rubber gloves, and take care not to inhale any fumes. After use thoroughly wash out utensils and wash your hands.

Used with care and respect, a modern insecticide can help you to grow clean, healthy plants. If the manufacturers instructions are not carried out, this can be courting disaster.

VIRUS

Virus remains little understood today either by the many Plant Quarantine Stations the world over, the many Plant Pathological Institutions, or the orchid growers themselves. The first indulge in heavy fumigations of Methyl-Bromide which is, at least in America, applied in a gaseous form with great care. Unfortunately in some countries without experience of this dangerous fumigant no regard is given to temperatures relative to density of the gas with the inevitable result that the plant is killed, thus easily eliminating the virus. The second body of men who have done so much in other plant diseases have wisely not pronounced as yet on virus which is so little understood. The average orchid grower however knows both the cause and the cure!

Cold, damp conditions where ventilation is lacking are

undoubtedly the prime cause of virus *coming to the surface*. Many of us think the disease inherent such as appendicitis in man. To eliminate it is at the moment impossible, but plants can be grown out of it by a little extra heat, ventilation and less root restriction.

The disease is also caused to take visibly bad proportions by excessive 'dunging' of the plant which seems to weaken the leaf cells. It is generally agreed that with Cymbidiums it is more common in Alexanderi g. 'Westonbirt' and its hybrids than in others. I have not noticed this, but I have seen a huge butch of Pauwelsii's badly affected and due only to manuring excessively. Alexanderi g. 'Westonbirt', however, invariably has virus and should a plant be acquired without virus one may be certain that it is not the true 'Westonbirt' F.C.C. variety.

Virus is rarely found in orchids as such but is unfortunately often found in collections of Cymbidiums, perhaps the most popular orchids. It is often referred to as Cymbidium Mosaic, or Black Streak Virus. Virus will rarely kill. If it gets too strong warm treatment will reduce it with each progressive new growth. Old leaves may be *stripped* off. It is most certainly spread by leaf-piercing insects, and in particular by red spider.

Quite a number of horticulturalists believe that virus is behind the variegation found in many forms of plant life. As variegated foliage can be most attractive, and *Cymbidium* Alexanderi g. 'Westonbirt' is certainly the finest parent ever raised by man, perhaps one might say that virus can be an asset! I have noticed in the past that a yellow striped Paphiopedilum, which might well have had virus, would not flower although so attractive to look at in leaf.

Do not use a knife. A knife will spread virus through the sap. In the U.S.A. Professor D. D. Jensen has proved it contagious through the sap, but not seedborne. Burn all virused leaves. Better still burn a virused plant. Isolate it anyway. In Cymbidiums it usually takes the form of transient flecking in the young leaves developing later into brown stripes.

Mosaic is much more common, particularly Cattleya leaf Mosaic, a form of Gloesporium. This ugly radiating circular mark will deface a plant, but not to my knowledge kill it. Do not confuse the purplish black markings associated with *Laelia purpurata* and *crispa* and their hybrids with leaf mosaic. It is a natural inherent and usually conspicuous marking which in no

49 *Angraecum sesquipedale*

50 *Dendrobium densiflorum*

51 *Epidendrum vitellinum*

52 *Cymbidium insigne* var. *sanderi*

53 *Cymbidium indigne* var. *sanderi*

54 *Angraecum infundibulare*

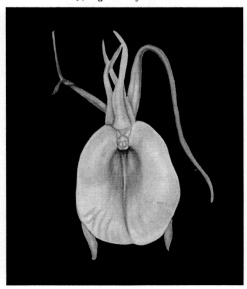

55 *Cymbidium* Sunrise (above)

56 *Cymbidium* 'Early' (right)

57 *Phalaenopsis schillerana*

58 *Epidendrum atropurpureum* var. *roseum*

59 *Phalaenopsis denevei*

61 *Cattleya* Fabulous

60 *Dendrobium atroviolaceum*

62 *Vandopsis parishi* var. *mariottiana*

63 *Paphiopedilum* 'Cameo'

64 *Dendrobium draconis*

65 *Paphiopedilum* 'Miracle Victory'

66 *Lycaste aromatica*

67 *Cattleya* 'Bill Dawson'

way affects growth or flower. Mosaic, is also frequently met with in Coelogynes, Lycastes, Lacaenas, Stanhopeas and other plicate leafed orchids.

There is another disease in the virus-fungoid group called, I believe, *Erwinia carotovora*, which is supposed to be prevalent in Cymbidiums in Australia. It has certainly not killed any at our nursery at Selsfield. It attacks the bulbs and, I am told, the edges of the leaves and sheaths around the bulbs, turning them brown, exuding sap and decay, but can be killed by antibiotic injections.

Common Cymbidium virus is recognised by the striated form it takes, and the transparency of the cells in the young growths before it hardens to brownish confluent markings. This Cymbidium virus staining of the leaves must not be confused with a similar looking light yellow, patchy marking which may well be caused by the young leaf having been burnt either by the insecticide or by the sun during an earlier stage of growth. This is easy to check for the mark remains constant and moves up with the growing leaf. Mosaic is usually blotch shaped and radiating with intervening spaces of clear green growth, the whole making a roundish shaped pattern up to 2 in. across.

Laelia albida

11

Selection of Plants

THE BEST selection of all is undoubtedly that made as a result of a combination of factors, intelligently correlated, and yet allowing for the personal taste and individuality of the amateur. Such factors are, in order of importance: (1) glasshouse space available; (2) minimum winter night temperature safely estimated; (3) aspects of house; (4) limit of financial investment, and (5) main object of hobby, namely (*a*) a botanical interest, (*b*) a desire to have plenty of seasonal cut flowers, (*c*) for exhibition purposes, (*d*) with a view to raising one's own seedlings, (*e*) a purely æsthetic reason for owning a plant, beautiful in itself, or finally (*f*) a real collector's love for the accumulation of *objects d'art*. Each constitutes a perfect excuse for spending one's surplus cash—little though that may be—on a grand hobby.

I suggest that if unable to visit a reputable orchid grower, you should begin with some of the following resistant subjects, forming as it were a 'barometrical' collection to test you out as to the greenness of your fingers.

CYMBIDIUM TRACYANUM or LOWIANUM. An Indian orchid, the former having chocolate striped scented flowers, the latter green flowers with brick red lips.

DENDROBIUM NOBILE. An Indian orchid with large amethyst and white flowers.

LAELIA ANCEPS. A Mexican orchid with mauve large flowers.

PAPHIOPEDILUM INSIGNE. An Indian slipper orchid, red–brown spotted.

ONCIDIUM ORNITHORYNCHUM. A Mexican orchid with shell pink small scented flowers in clusters.

ODONTOGLOSSUM PULCHELLUM. A Mexican orchid with pure white scented orange blossom like flowers.

Selecting an orchid from a nursery can be as thrilling to a plantsman as buying a hat is to a lady. I should perhaps add that those who are limited by space or the lack of a garden to buying orchids for culture indoors or in a tiny greenhouse or frame, should refer to Chapter 7 on Indoor Culture for a further selection of miniatures. We are now specialising in miniature Cymbidiums, which make wonderful table centres.

The following Orchids are some of many which we can sincerely recommend for beginners:

Maxillaria picta—cream and porphyry red, scented.

Paphiopedilum venustum—long lasting, mottled leaves, green and purple flowers.

Oncidium flexuosum—small, brilliant yellow flowers, on long spikes.

Paphiopedilum insigne sanderae—yellow and white, November flowering, and they last six weeks.

Cymbidium hybrid—a named variety, choice of many colours.

Paphiopedilum hirsutissimum—brown, green and mauve, last 8 weeks in flower.

Odontoglossum crispum hybrid—large white flowers spotted rose/mauve, and purple or yellow in sprays.

Odontioda hybrid—rich red-purple flowers in sprays.

Maxillaria nigrescens

12

Hybridising and Seed Raising

~~~~~~~~~~~~~~~~~~~~~~~~~~~~~

THE HYBRIDISING of orchids is a constant source of interest and hope for the future—in fact I think it helps to keep one going, for even with 100 per cent success in sowing, from five to ten years are required for each generation!

I do not intend revising any of the matter that follows as it still applies, I believe, 100 per cent, but I would like to make the additional remarks that follow in the next paragraph.

I have done little laboratory work for the past five years, but I have learnt quite a considerable amount by meeting people and discussing their ways of raising orchids from seed. It remains a very precise job of work, and one requiring concentration and plenty of time. There have been put forward in the past five years many articles and suggestions regarding media to be used and the manner of mixing it. The best suggestion I have heard of and one which certainly works with a neighbour of mine is so simple as to seem unbelievable. It is that the mixture should consist of only agar, fish emulsion, and an antibiotic fungicide. Obviously other things may be added if wished, but these three do certainly suffice in the case of my friend's cultures.

It would be more practical for the average amateur with hopes of producing his own hybrid to limit his action to the thoughtful selection of the pod and pollen parents, and the actual transference by means of a clean bone or wooden pencil of the pollen from the one chosen parent to the stigmatic surface of the other. In most orchids this takes the form of a viscid concave space immediately beneath the pollen anthers and cap, always found on the top of the column which is a continuation of the ovary in the epicentre of the flower. The pollen is conglomerated into two, four, six or eight little bundles attached by anthers to the column, and easily handled as the anthers have a sticky base.

The choice of parents depends on many factors. Haphazard crossing of flowers is to be deprecated. First of all study the affinity of the two species and/or hybrids you propose to cross. This is far greater in orchids than is generally known—proof? Several quadrigeneric hybrids such as Potinaria. Thus though you might reasonably try a cross of great theoretical promise such as a Zygopetalum with a Bifrenaria, your chances of success are very remote. Often even in one Genus two distinct species will not give seed, e.g., *Odontoglossum pulchellum* with *Odontoglossum grande*. Hybridising is always a gamble and often a thrilling one! Choose carefully, and with an inward eye to potential results. If you want to create something new—well then you must study the International Register (Sanders List of Orchid Hybrids—one of the two oldest study books extant).

Having successfully made the cross a few days or weeks will suffice for an appreciable swelling of the ovary to become visible, and the pod thus forming can be left for six (for some orchids, such as Vandas) to ten months, when it will usually change colour, yellowing, and will show signs of splitting along the placenta.

Harvest the seed in a clean polythene or ordinary tissue paper bag. The viable seed may be as few as a dozen, or as many as a million or two. I once counted on a proportional basis nearly three million seeds in a 5 in. pod of *Cymbidium tracyanum* (see pages 57, 58 and 59).

This is where I suggest your worries end and you visit your nearest or dearest commercial orchid grower, and leave the growing pains and worries of symbiotic or asymbiotic culture to *him*! He will usually help you out and raise a few for a nominal charge, or if *he* considers the seed desirable, on a fifty–fifty basis.

Symbiosis and symbiotic culture. Symbiosis, a mutual digestion, I like to call it, takes place in nearly all plant rooting systems, it is now generally agreed, and we are indebted in the first place to A. B. Frank in 1885 for the discovery and study of this most essential and happy relationship between minute fungal growths (mycorrhizal growths) and the host plant, whereby the mycorrhiza feeds on natural traces and digests them before passing them on to the host. Subsequently at the turn of the nineteenth century Bernard (French), Bugeff (German), Ramsbottom (English), and Knudson (American), contributed enormously to our present practical knowledge. This symbiotic action, we have satisfied ourselves, is almost spontaneous, and need not be artificially stimulated by pure cultures, even for the minute plantules found in Erlenmeyer flasks in the orchid laboratories up and down the country. Perhaps one day it will be proven, as I am sure it must, that these fungi *are already* present in the seed germ, provided in some miraculous way by nature under Divine Providence.

It was Dr Lewis Knudson of Cornell University who, shortly after the 1914–18 war, suspected the action of mycorrhyzal growths releasing carbohydrates and nitrogenous substances from the growing medium, aided in practice by the addition of various sugars to the solutions used.

And now we come to the seed which is viable more or less in proportion to the complications of the genetical relationship of the chosen parents. Those nearest to the 'God-made' species usually give the greater proportion of viable seed: those most complicated multigenerics the lesser. The seed is infinitely small—smaller than ground pepper in many cases—and is accordingly difficult to sterilise and tend.

It has been computed by no less a person than Charles Darwin, that if one of our common British orchids attained 100 per cent fertility, and conditions were 100 per cent ideal, then in the first generation one plant would ensure a full acre of progeny; in the second generation the U.K. would be covered, and in the third, the whole world! Orchid seed contains protoplasm as against the usual embryonic plantule in most seeds. If you must store or hold over temporarily seed or pollen, I suggest you do so in small glass phials, well corked. Wedge beneath a small wad of cotton wool, a few grains of calcium chloride. A minute spot of glycerine may be dropped with advantage on to the cotton wool before insertion. After inserting seed, do not forget a slip of paper with the names of the parents. Keep the phial in a cool dark place: a refrigerator will do—but not in the ice box.

Asymbiotic Cultures. The asymbiotic cultures (*non* symbiotic, i.e., no inoculation of pure cultures of fungi into growing media) reduce the hazards of nature enormously. By comparison with the old-fashioned orchidist's practice of sowing on parent plants (prepared surfaces) the newer asymbiotic culture is a vast

102

stride—but!—even today we find that stronger quicker growing plantlets are produced by sowing on well-rooted parent plants than those from the same seed pod raised in the laboratory flasks. In the case of Paphiopedilums, I estimate the difference in terms of time as 12–18 months gain. Turkish towelling, and finely-cut osmunda surfaces were and still are used successfully in specially heated frames.

If, having read the following paragraphs, you revert to the preceding paragraphs, I have no doubt you will want to ask several questions concerning the successful raising of seedlings on parent plants, and here is the answer to at least some of them.

There is a very good plastic pot on the market with transparent and well ventilated plastic cover which exactly fits the base. We have more recently used these very successfully with sterilised sphagnum compost for the sowing of such seed as Disa, keeping the plastic pots well covered in a well heated frame for a long as 3 months before inspecting for germination of seed. The sphagnum retains its moisture sufficiently throughout this and even longer periods when kept in well shaded positions.

The plant should be of the same genus as the plants from which the seed is taken or of an allied genera. The parent plant chosen to be used for sowing should be picked out in the late autumn months from amongst those that show considerable root action on and near the surface. The surface will undoubtedly be found to be a little green and rough if it has been potted in the normal way, and must therefore be teated as follows: With a sharp pointed stick carefully clean away the top ¼ in. or so of compost, taking particular notice of algae and ferns. The thus broken up surface should not involve disturbing the roots. Spray it very lightly with an insecticide. Prepare a new surface by carefully re-surfacing with a fine grade of pure bark.

When the days lengthen, the seed having been kept in a cool dry place if collected in the autumn, choose a bright sunny day and very carefully picking up an infinitely small quantity at the end of a clean label, tap the label in such a manner over the surface of the plant as to deposit the seed fairly evenly. The label should be held about an inch above the surface and one should not breathe heavily as the seed is, as I have stressed before, finer than pepper. The plant must now be placed in a well protected corner of the staging with a glass frame over it or polythene in such a manner as to prevent any water being applied to the surface except by capillary action. In other words, the plant is watered by being placed in a bowl or pan of water. It is a good thing to have a pinguicula nearby to collect any of the small flies that do eat seed and seedlings.

Applied Asymbiotic Culture. Before you start such cultures, choose a clean corner of your greenhouse, kitchen or bathroom, and buy, acquire or make the following essentials:

A pint of pure alcohol, a small carboy of distilled water, a very small quantity of picric acid and mercury bichloride (for sterilising stoppers), a tiny bottle each of phosphoric and hydrochloric acid HCL/10 and small glass stoppered jars of: calcium nitrate, calcium hypochlorite (for sterilising seed), potassium–dihydrogen phosphate, magnesium sulphate, phosphate of iron and ammonium sulphate. (The calcium hypochlorite loses its power quickly when unstopped, and might well be replaced by a proprietary brand such as Chloros, which is a liquid.)

An acid testing outfit is essential. (Accurate ones are costly.) Cotton wool, a pair of forceps, or preferably two (one small and one large); twelve test tubes and stand for them; twelve Erlenmeyer 250 cc. flasks or twelve suitable narrow–necked bottles of the same capacity are needed. Blotter-filters are necessary and a glass stirring rod, a pipette, and an eye dropper. Essential is a large 1,000 cc. and smaller 50–100 cc. glass measure, and less essential, silver paper and rubber bands to finally seal off the flasks, or tubed rubber stoppers. A metric scale (quite inexpensive second–hand), a Bunsen burner and a gas ring (or electric plate), a platinum needle for the actual sowing, which can be bent and flattened by heat into a glass handle. A kitchen earthenware bowl and a common washing-up basin are also needed, but finally, alas! the most expensive of all is another *must*, namely an auto-clave. However, a pressure cooker costs less and can be used.

Because of the enormous number of fungi, algae, bacteria in the air, in your breath, in fact everywhere, you *must* work 100 per cent aseptically. I suggest, apart from clean surrounds in the immediate vicinity of your 'pseudo-lab', that you do all the sowing with rubber gloves over a steaming basin of water—

hence the gas ring and washing–up basin in list of pre-requisites!—always holding the open flask inclined downwards over the hot rising air.

The formulas suggested below for the make–up of the media are deliberately chosen for their simplicity and could, of course, be elaborated considerably. They are essentially good ones and have given successful results the world over. Withner in his book, *The Orchids, a Scientific Survey,* gives no less than 35 formulas.

KNUDSON BURGEFF formula, solution B (1922)

Monopotassium acid phosphate	KH_2PO_4	0.25	grms.
Calcium nitrate	$Ca(NO_3)_2.4H_2O$	1.00	,,
Ammonium sulphate	$(NH_4)_2SO_4$	0.50	,,
Magnesium sulphate	$Mg\ SO_4.7H_2O$	0.25	,,
Ferric phosphate	$FeSO_4.7H_2O$	0.05	,,
Sucrose		20.00	,,
Agar		17.50	,,
Distilled water		1,000	ml.

Acidity should be adjusted to pH5 with hydrochloric acid.

LA GARDE (1929)

Magnesium sulphate	$Mg\ SO_4.7H_2O$	1.00	grms.
Calcium nitrate	$Ca(NO_3)_2.4H_2O$	1.00	,,
Monopotassium sulphate	KH_2SO_4	1.00	,,
Calcium chloride	$CaCl_2$	1.00	,,
Ammonium nitrate	NH_4NO_2	0.50	,,
Ammonium carbonite	$(NH_4)_2CO_3.H_2O$	0.50	,,
Ferous phosphate	$FePO_4$	0.33	,,
Sugar		20.00	,,
Agar		17.50	,,
Distilled water		1,000	mil.

Acidity should be adjusted to 4.8/5.1.

Knudson's Solution is often modified as follows:

>   cut out:
>
> Fe PO4 (phosphate of iron)
>   add:
>
> K2 HPO4 0.25 gms. (potassium phosphate)
> 1 cc. of 5 per cent solution of phosphate of iron
> 10 ccs. hydrochloric acid N/10
> 1 drop phosphoric acid

To make a safe and first class aseptic stopper, mix into alcohol (industrial spirit) a solution of picric acid and mercuric bichloride, *working with rubber gloves*. In *liquid* form this solution is dangerous if applied to the skin (15 drachms picric acid and 15 drachms mercuric bichloride to 2 litres of industrial spirit).

Steep an unfolded 2 lb. roll of cotton wool into the solution which should go yellow, then squeeze out the surplus which can be used for more cotton wool. Dry in trays in the sun. When dry, pull into puffs large enough to form firm stoppers to the necks of your sowing flasks.

Having measured out all the ingredients of the chosen formula, mix in the following order to reduce precipitation to a minimum, taking care to dissolve each chemical thoroughly before mixing. First dissolve the agar, sucrose and warm distilled water, subsequently adding the mixture of the five following constituents:

>   1st calcium nitrate
>   2nd ammonium sulphate
>   3rd magnesium sulphate
>   4th monopotassium acid phosphate
>   5th ferric–phosphate

Adjust acidity of the final concoction to a reaction of between pH 4.8 and 5.0 by the use of a few drops of either Chloros (to make more alkaline) or N/10 HCL acidity. Autoclave the whole for 20 minutes at 15 lb. pressure. Leave to cool slightly and pour out into the flasks. It is usual to work on a basis of 1,000 cc., thus you would have from 80 to 90 cc. for each of the twelve flasks, which quantity of medium pour in. Re-autoclave the solution now in twelve bottles at 15 lb. for 20 minutes, raising the

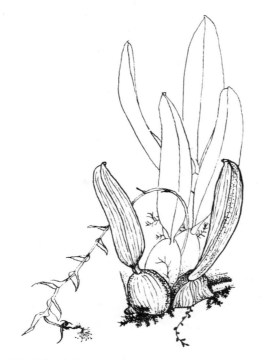

Bulbophyllum barbigerum

pressure to the maximum conducive with safety for 2 further minutes. This will ensure precipitation of a certain amount of liquid on the solution when solidified. Lay the flasks out on their sides with their necks on a bar of wood, so that the flask mouth is 1 in. or so off the table, thus allowing the media to settle and solidify over a maximum area parallel to the axis of the flask. When cool, the flasks are ready to sow—usually within 12 hours. Never leave them for more than 12 days before use.

Sowing. The seed should be shaken up in Chloros (1 in 20 dist. H_2O) for 10 minutes in small test-tubes. To transfer seed to the flasks a platinum needle should be used for Paphiopedilums and Cymbidiums, and a dropper for Cattleya type seed—in this case the chloros in the test-tube should be diluted with sterilised dist. H_2O or Chloros 1–60. The sowing operation must be performed over a steaming bowl and droppers and needles sterilised in Chloros. Rubber gloves must be worn by the operator, who must also be careful not to breathe too heavily on the flasks when sowing. The mouth of the flask should never be allowed to point upwards. With a little practice these operations can be done neatly and efficiently with little risk of contamination.

Seal down with the cotton wool stoppers firmly, and neatly cover with silver paper and rubber rings to ensure that dirt is not applied to the wool stoppers when handling during the next six months.

After sowing, place the flasks immediately in a warm frame (from 70 to 80° F. (21–26° C.)), keeping it 80 per cent humid by day, which will ensure 100 per cent humidity by night when the temperature drops (and must do so) thus drawing the air in and out through the sterilised stoppers, an induction which naturally results.

Usually 4–6 months are sufficient for manageable plants to be trans-flasked, specially if you can sow in the months of December/January and 'prick off' on to community pots or trays of fine bark during the following spring.

13

Contrivances that Ensure the Fertilisation of Orchids

~~~~~~

THERE ARE very many other weird and wonderful orchids that are worth acquiring if only to study the various devices nature has evolved to ensure their fertilisation.

One of the most extraordinary orchids I have seen is *Caleana major*. This orchid is known as Australia's "Flying Duck Orchid" which is fertilised by a fly known in Latin as *Phyrotona leachi*. For a full description of this wonderful orchid I strongly recommend you read page 668 of the American Orchid Society Bulletin for August 1968. Briefly, the labellum is so sensitive that the insect is thrown back into the cavity formed by the wings of the column, lying there for some 15 to 20 seconds before recovering sufficiently to make its escape during which it removes the pollinia or at least some of it, brushing it on to the sigmatic surface. Some 20 minutes later the labellum suddenly jerks back into its normal position.

CORYANTHES MACRANTHA

THESE FLOWERS are among the most wonderful in the orchid world, remarkable both for their size and extraordinary structure. They are carried in descending spikes. The sepals and petals, 2–3 in. long, are rather narrow, thin in texture and fade quickly. The lip is thick, fleshy, wax-like in texture and curiously constructed. A short stalk is produced from the base of the column inclined upward and outwards, the wing-like sepals and petals being curved in the opposite direction. This short stalk ends in a cup or hood-like process, which at right angles gives rise to a second stalk or column-like process, which in turn expands into a second, much larger cup or bucket, so shaped and placed as to catch a liquid secreted by two short horns or knobs at the base of the column (as much as a fluid ounce). The flowers are strongly odorous and insects (usually a small bee) are attracted both by the scent and the tissue under the hood. In their endeavours to feed on this they fall into the bucket and in their struggles to escape from the flowers are forced to use the stair-way like structure at the back. Over this aperture the pollinia are placed and must therefore adhere to the insect's head as it forces its way out. Pollination is thus ensured when the bee visits the next flower.

MASDEVALLIA MUSCOSA

The is another quite wonderful miniature orchid with a very hirsute slender wiry stem some 6–8 in. high topped with a yellow flower about a centimetre across. It is *most* intriguing. Should you put even a hair on to the centre of the lip and thus disturb it, the lip will close to with a motion which is most interesting to watch! It starts off at 0 miles per hour, so to speak, and gradually accelerates ending with a *'clip'*. The lip is so beautifully boat-shaped that it exactly fits against the column and makes an almost watertight compartment in which is the poor struggling small insect that fertilizes the flower. Some 30 minutes later the lip will drop open again to release the insect, with the pollen of course carried by it, to be attracted by another flower which in due course it will fertilize.

MORMODES

This extraordinary orchid was once described to me by a rather cynical member of the Diplomatic Corps as the 'French Diplomat'. This extraordinary orchid is most bizarre in its form and also its colouring. It often has one sexed flowers quite distinct from the other sexed flowers, but what makes it so unique is the fact that if you take an axis anywhere no two parts of the perianth ever form a symmetrical pattern! The lip sepals and petals are all contorted.

ANGRAECUM SESQUIPEDALE

This orchid has such historical interest that anyone who has read Darwin's *Fertilisation of Orchids* will not want to read the next lines. I must tell you, however, that the orchid is featured in the Natural History Museum in Kensington and featured by a coloured plate from my Grandfather's monumental work 'The

Reichenbachia'. Against the stone-litho is a night flying moth of huge dimensions. This extraordinary orchid has a nectary some 18 in. along—hence the Latin name—and to be fertilised Darwin decided in the Victorian era that there must be a night-flying moth—the flower is white and scented—which has a probosis 18 in. long. Imagine the disbelief of his contemporaries! In fact, after his death the moth was discovered and it had an 18 in. probosis operated very much like a Christmas cracker which, when blown out extends. It is worth a visit to the Natural History Museum to see this moth and the life-size picture from my Grandfather's book, in the main entrance hall.

OPHRYS APIFERA

The Bee Orchid. This orchid has a labellum which suggests in no small way the body of a bee and is in fact fertilised by a bee. I have once in my life seen this orchid wild in an area which I dare not mention for it is now so rare.

CATASETUM

This genus of orchid is quite extraordinary. The flowers are sometimes bi-sexual and sometimes have a male flower and a female produced from separate bulbs from the same or different plants. The interest in this orchid lies in its manner of self reproduction which is unique. The pollinia (pollen masses) are attrached to the column in such a manner that a tendril running down the column curves into the flat space of the labellum ending in a fine spiral filament. Touch the filament what e'er insect you be and away flies the pollinia at speed estimated by various botanists at from 20 to 30 miles per hour! This exciting orchid has a placenta of viscous matter enclosed in a rhomboid capsule which adheres to the column (central and sex part of the orchid) in such a manner that the attachment is so knife-edge fine that the touching of the tendril by any insect or extraneous factor causes the fine edges to this placenta to break away outwards from the base and allow the air to enter, which air immediately solidifies the liquid causing a contraction of the capsule which springs the pollinia away from the column at speed. I defy any engineer, electronic or otherwise, to imitate this extraordinary mechanism which to me points out, in my perhaps simple-minded approach to the subject, the clear possibility of there

111

being an Almighty power who designed such plants. Possibly the same Power that designed the incredible beauty of the atom which can be used to such dis- or ad-vantage.

I could continue the list of extraordinary orchids fertilised in the most ingenious manners to include many more pages, but I will end with a last example which may well involve me in considerable correspondence with botantists and plantsmen and orchidists, a risk I am willingly taking. I am referring now to *Arachnanthe lowii*. This extraordinary plant which I have seen in flower at Glasnevin with a spike some 8 or 9 ft long can produce spikes as long as 12 ft. They are pendant and very showy. The flowers are large, being some 3 to 4 in. across. The first flowers, that is from the top of the pendant spike are of a certain colouring, the median flowers being slightly different and the basal flowers *completely* different. The top flowers are male and provided with pollinia, the next flowers seem to be neutral and at the lower end are the female flowers. This plant, is I think, fertilised by large ants which carry the pollen from the top of the spike down to the bottom, and in the course of the long journey invariably deposit some of them on the stigmatic surfaces of the basal *female* flowers. This sounds like phantasy but could well be fact. The inference that I like to refer to occasionally is that the female flowers are below and the male above! I am in no way suggesting that this proves the superiority of the human male!

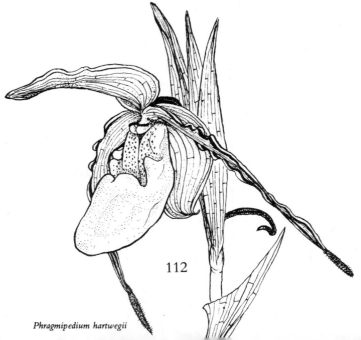

Phragmipedium hartwegii

112

14

Monthly Operations

THESE NOTES cannot be followed literally because differences in locality, in the state of the plants, the weather conditions and the outside temperatures must all be taken into consideration.

The temperatures for the cool house are as for Odontoglossums. Where these are not present in the cool division, but only Cymbidiums, hard bulbed Oncidiums, etc., and resting plants, occasional falls of a further 5 or 7° F. (3 or 4° C.) will do no harm.

Temperatures

January	Day		Night
Cool House .... 55° F.(12–13° C.)			50° F. (10° C.)
Intermediate House ...60° F. (15–16° C.)	or more	58–60° F. (14–16° C.)
Warm House .... 70° F. (21° C.)			65–70° F. (18–21° C.)

The foregoing and following temperatures must be regarded as approximate. They should be worked to as nearly as possible, but outdoor weather will cause a certain amount of fluctuation.

Little can be done in this month. If the weather is mild, Paphiopedilums, the flowers of which have been cut off, may be re-potted with advantage. On no account pot any of the warmer-growing orchids, and specially not Vandas. Damping must be regulated according to the weather, and the pipe heat used. In the cool house one damping should be sufficient. In none of the houses should superfluous moisture be present at night. Damping should be done with a rising temperature and never after lunch time.

The pipe heat used in all sections during this and the previous month will often encourage thrips so that occasional fumigation may be necessary. It is safer during this season than spraying. Shading, unless the locality is exceptional, will not be required.

Watering possibly requires more thought in this month than any other. To Paphiopedilums, Masdevallias and bulbless kinds, it is a necessity, but root action is not nearly so vigorous and even with them, judgment must be used. Hard bulbed kinds, like *Oncidium tigrinum, Odontoglossum grande,* at rest in the cool house, will probably go through the month without water. Plants which require water must not be watered so frequently as to induce 'sogginess' in the compost.

In the intermediate house the same remarks apply. If winter growths are present, as they often are on Cattleya hybrids, err rather on the dry side as regards watering.

Heavier damping and more frequent waterings can be given in the warm house than in the other sections. Plants standing in corners, or in proximity to the hot-water pipes, should be looked at frequently.

Airing in the cool division, air in suitable weather; usually bottom air is sufficient to change the atmosphere without losing moisture and warmth, but top air can often be given for short periods when the sun is out.

In the intermediate house, top air can seldom or never be used, but again the atmosphere can be revitalised by the use of bottom air, when possible or by the use of an electric fan. The same applies to the warm house, but to a lesser degree.

Night condensation of moisture occurs in some houses. It is particularly damaging when it rests on plicate-leaved orchids, e.g., Lycastes, and any flowers which may open. Usually its presence indicates too much moisture in the house late in the day.

The syringing of plants should be avoided. Keep temperatures and conditions as consistent as possible, and avoid draughts. Potting material, ready for use, should be prepared or acquired. This month and February are ideal for cheching up on pests and disease. Handle each plant individually, and check under the pots for slugs and silvertails. Artificial light from 3–10 p.m. is useful.

February

Temperatures at night should be much as for the last month, but the increased sun power will cause a rise in the day temperature. Effort should be made not to allow the night temperatures to fall below the minimums given.

Airing may be followed much as in the last month, but often in

114

the cool house it may be given for longer periods. Bright, sunny days with cold winds are especially dangerous.

Paphiopedilums out of flower with advanced growths may be potted, as may Cymbidiums, which are not in spike and have growths.

Early-flowered Dendrobiums may be potted towards the end of the month, but to the amateur, with the accomodation of but one house, we suggest deferring any potting until March and early April.

As the month wanes, so still higher temperatures may be obtained in the day. Corresponding changes must be made with damping, airing, firing, etc., but the weather is usually too changeable for any consistency to be advised. Each day brings its own requirements.

In all the houses, if opportunity occurs, sponge and clean any plants that require it.

Resting orchids—Oncidiums, Cattleyas, *Laelia anceps* and its allies, etc.—should be looked at at least once a week. The increased day temperatures and possibly extra pipe heat, used during this and the last month, may have induced a tendency to shrivel. At the first sign of this the plant or plants should be thoroughly watered. Blinds should be overhauled and put into position. Artificial light from 3–10 p.m. is useful.

March

Although cold winds and frosts are often present in this month, the sun is rapidly gaining power and the day temperatures rise considerably, though of comparitively short duration, and are often followed by a cold night. Damping must be in accordance, and always before lunchtime. We rarely damp down later than 11 a.m. in the winter months, and noon in March, especially if the temperatures are expected to fall in the night or very early morning; it must be so arranged that though the atmosphere is not really dry at night, and the floors and walls remain damp, visible moisture is not present in the morning. In some localities damping down may have to be done twice a day and, if the weather is bright, it should be thoroughly done; on suitable days, saturate the floors, walls and stage. Drying winds, sunshine, and the necessary fire heat often make this one of the most difficult months in the year from the point of view of keeping the moisture conditions correct.

In the early part of the month it is often difficult to maintain temperatures, but less difficulty is usually experienced towards its end. Occasional falls to February temperatures will occur, but a slight increase by day and night is desirable.

Cool house, 55–60° F. (12–15° C.) by day; 50–53° F. (10–12° C.) by night. Intermediate-house, 65–70° F. (18–21° C.) by day; 60–65° F. (15–18° C.) by night. Warm house, 70–75° F. (21–24° C.) by day; night as near 70° F. (21° C.) as possible, but not above that figure.

The day temperatures will often be exceeded on sunny days.

Shading. It must be remembered that young growths, if present, are comparatively tender. Though shading is necessary, it should be removed in the afternoon, fairly early, particularly in the warm and intermediate houses, so that the sun heat may be conserved into the late afternoon and evening. In the cool house shading may remain longer, but even there a benefit is obtained from sun heat in the afternoon. The times to remove blinds must be governed by position, locality and weather. Err rather on the light side than the shady.

Potting may be proceeded with on plants in any division which show signs of activity.

Ventilation requires thought, particularly when cold winds and bright sunshine occur together. Do not ventilate too freely for the sake of lowering temperature. You lose moisture and risk draughts. Control pipe heat, if possible, and give an extra damp in the afternoons. Pipe heat is unlikely to be needed at all in the daytime this month unless the outside temperatures are exceptionally low.

The Odontoglossum house, in particular, should be kept as consistent as possible. If necessary, shade a little earlier in the day to prevent increased temperature; 50–55° F. (10–12° C.) at night, and 55–60° F (12–15° C.) by day.

April

Temperatures should be as for March.

The cool house, 60–65° F. (15–18°C.) by day; 55° F. (12–13° C.) or near, by night. Intermediate house, 65–70° F. (18–21° C.) by day; 60–65° F. (15–18° C.) at night. Warm house, about 70–75° F. (21–24° C.) by day; 70° F. (21° C.) at night.

All will rise higher by sun heat in the day.

Re-potting should be carried on in all divisions and genera. Damping should be increased and the syringe may gradually be brought into general use. In the cool division and the Odontoglossum house, pipe heat can often be dispensed with entirely in the day, but is usually not safe to shut it off entirely.

Shading must be in position earlier and removed a little later. The intermediate and warm houses may be closed as the sun declines, and the sun heat conserved. If the damping is properly effected, a film of moisture will be present on the glass, which will prevent scorching, the blinds being rolled up after damping, in the late afternoon.

The cool division should not be closed as early as the warm and intermediate; a slightly increased temperature does no harm, but tropical heat should be avoided.

Watering may be indulged in more liberally, but it is advisable to allow plants with short growths and little root action to get moderately dry between waterings.

May

The majority of the plants will by now have been re-potted, but the conflicting habits of hybrids, particularly among Cattleyas, causes their potting season to extend through this month and often into the next. This is the month ehen you can remove offsets and kakees (baby plants or axilliary growths) from the vandacious orchids and pot them up on their own, always providing each offset has a minimum of one or two live roots. Summer weather is now more assured and temperatures should, in the cool house, be 55–60° F. (12–15° C.) at night; 60° F. (15–16° C.) or more by day. In the intermediate, 65–70° F. (18–21° C.), or slightly higher, by night; 70–80° F. (21–26° C.) in the day. The warm house 70–75° F. (21–24° C.) by night, but may run up to 90° F. (32° C.) by day.

The Odontoglossum house should be kept about 60° F. (15–16° C.) at night, or rather less, and as little as possible more by day. Shut the houses up in the afternoon, as advised in April, but slightly later. Usually pipes may be entirely shut off from the cool and Odontoglossum houses and controlled in both the intermediate and warm. Watering and syringing can be indulged in quite freely. Night air may be admitted to the cool and

Odontoglossum house whenever outside conditions allow.

June and July

These months require practically a continuation of the May treatment, with a slight increase in damping, watering and syringing. Pipes can usually be disused in the intermediate division entirely, and often for varying periods in the warm division.

In the Odontoglossum house difficulty may be experienced in keeping temperatures down. Shading must be carefully considered. It may be necessary at the very beginning of the month to stipple the glass even though heavy wooden blinds are in use. This stippling may be washed off in September. Even with Odontoglossums it is better to have an increased day temperature with moisture, rather than a lower temperature and a dry atmosphere. It is usually quite safe to leave ventilators open through the night and so compensate for the extra heat of the day.

Night air to a lesser degree is often beneficial in the intermediate house. Bottom air may be given with discretion to the warm house at night, and occasionally by the top ventilators, outside conditions permitting. In the cool house with Cymbidiums, Oncidiums, hard-bulbed Odontoglossums, Lycastes, etc., air may be left on at night, but an increased temperature in the late afternoon in often beneficial.

All potting should be finished by the end of June.

August

The first part of this month is often a continuation of July, but the nights are shorter and tend to become slightly cooler, though by day the sun is often as hot as in July; often apparently more so after a dry spell.

In all sections the majority of plants are approaching maturity, but water must still be given with freedom. Plants must be helped as much as possible to complete their growths and make solid, well-finished pseudo bulbs. Water is still very necessary as, if withheld too soon, Cattleyas and Dendrobiums will be inclined to shrivel.

During the latter part of the month, outside, early-morning conditions must be studied, though there is little risk of undue

118

falls in temperature. Usually it is risky to admit night air by the top ventilators in the warm house, but by the bottom ventilators it can still be admitted particularly in the Paphiopedilum house or division. In the intermediate, air should still be given at the top, and perhaps in conjunction with bottom air at night. Blinds should be drawn up earlier and pulled down later and more top air given in the day with discretion, and with thought to the hardening of the plant. In the cool and Odontoglossum houses conditions will remain much as in July; slight falls in temperature towards morning will benefit.

Many plants, in fact, most of the bulbous orchids will have made up their bulbs and require very much less water. This is the month when you begin seriously to expose your Cymbidiums—those with mature bulbs—to direct light. It is essential to ripen these plants if flower spikes are to be ensured. The leaves must not be allowed, however, to become yellow, but rather a yellowish green. Those large Cymbidiums which have in the past yeats proved reluctant to flower may now be put out of doors in light shade, e.g., under an apple tree.

September

Particularly as the month progresses, the inside temperature must be reduced slightly as the nights are longer and colder. In the cool and Odontoglossum houses the night temperature may fall to 55 or 50° F. (12 or 10° C.); night air may still be left on with advantage, provided the minimum temperature is maintained. In the intermediate house, the night temperature should be from 60 to 65° F. (15–18° C.) and the day temperature should be 70–75° F. (21–24° C.); less without sun. The warm house will still go over 80° F. (26° C.) on sunny days, but should be kept at 70° F. (21° C.) by night, or slightly higher.

Watering must still be continued, but not as frequently as in the summer.

Damping in all divisions must still continue, but the time of the afternoon, or early evenings, damping must be advanced according to conditions. The boiler will be required for the warm house and for the intermediate, but not for the cool division. Syringing must be practised with more care, moisture must not lodge in the leaf axils or similiar places through the night. Re-potting from the end of this month, with the exception

119

of Odontoglossums, should be avoided if possible but, if time permits, give an 'overhaul' to each plant; clean, if insect pests are suspected, and renovate any weak places in the composts. Air should be admitted whenever conditions allow, and the blinds removed earlier. Extra light sill now benefit most plants in all sections. September and October are ideal months for re-potting those Odontoglossums which are in the right stage of growth and, or course, *require* re-potting.

Catasetums, Acinetas, or any similiar plants which have matured early may be removed to the intermediate division.

A very slight purplish hue may appear on Odontoglossums, Miltonias, etc., and indicates the process of ripening. Cattleyas, etc., show the effect of their slightly hardened leaves and bulbs. The Burmese Dendrobiums are benefited by greater exposure to light when their growths are completely finished as they should be by now.

A command of heat may be desirable in the cool divisions by the end of this month. Cymbidiums must now be given direct light throughout the day, and flower spikes should already be visible coming up from the sides of the leading bulbs. They are easily distinguished from leaf growths by their roundness and their stubby tips. Leaf growths are pointed.

This is the month when you should thoroughly check your heating apparatus and clean boilers and tools, and oil heaters, electric pumps, fans, etc. It is also the month when you should wash off most of the shading which has been applied by brush. Usually in this country this is done by the rain, but it is desirable to clean the house neatly on the outside, stopping the water inlet to the tank with a ball of rag, and running the lime filled water resulting from the washing down of the house into a path or bed alongside the house.

October

Fire heat is usually required in the cool and Odontoglossum houses. In both, a gentle heat often allows the admission of more air, and in any case prevents any approach to stagnancy in the atmosphere; fire heat must be very carefully given to Odontoglossums, but they cannot grow in a very low temperature. The day temperature for the cool houses should be 60° F. (15–16° C.) or slightly more, but at night it may be 55° F. (12–13° C.) or a shade lower. September and October are ideal months for re-potting those Odontoglossums which are in the right stage of growth and, of course, *require* re-potting.

The intermediate house, 65–70° F. (18–21° C.) by day, and 65° F. (18° C.) or rather less at night. The warm house should be kept near 70° F. (21° C.) at night, and rise 5° F. (3° C.) by day, or more.

Damping must be reduced, twice a day is usual, or may be more than sufficient, but on suitable daus see that at least one damping is very thorough. The outside atmosphere is usually much more humid than during the previous month. The same reasoning must be applied to watering but, even with plants which appear quite matured, it is not wise to withhold it entirely.

In the warm house care must be taken to avoid leaving water on the foliage overnight. Though most of the inmates benefit by exposure to light, the greater number hardly require the amount given to Cattleyas, Dendrobiums, etc.

The roller blinds may usually be safely removed and stored at the end of this month.

November

Temperatures should be much as for last month, but with the advent of cold weather, slight falls may be allowed in all divisions.

Though the month is often humid, damp cold often prevails, and more pipe heat is required. Damping must be regulated by this, in conjunction with outside conditions. Extra pipe heat means extra damping, perhaps twice a day, but neither plants nor houses should be unduly damp in the early mornings.

Should fogs be experienced, all the divisions should be kept closed; endeavour to maintain an even temperature, and avoid excess of water, though the houses must not be allowed to become aridly dry. A slight fall in all the temperatures is perhaps better than too much heat. Examine the plants for insects. This month and December are ideal for tying up and re-staging your orchids. November is the month to begin artificial light from 3–10 p.m. until end February.

December

The temperatures for this month should approximate 70–75° F. (21–24° C.) by day in the warm house, and 70° F. (21° C.), or nearly so, at night. The intermediate house, 60–65° F. (15–18° C.) by day, and 60° F. (15–16° C.) at night. The cool house 60° F. (15–16° C.) by day, and 50–55° F. (10–12° C.) by night; all slightly lower if sharp frosts or cold winds occur.

In cool houses where only such plants as Cymbidiums and hard-bulbed winter-resting plants like *Oncidium tigrinum, varicosum, Odontoglossum grande* and *citrosmum,* etc., are grown, the night temperature may fall to 45° F. (7° C.).

Do not water over-much this month. In the case of matured plants, waterings will only be required once a fortnight. Seedlings, however, in the warmer houses will require looking over at least twice a week.

Miltonia spectabilis

15

Collection and Importation

~~~~~~~~~~~~~~~~~~~~~~~~~~

IT WILL be seen from the Appendices A, B and C that follow, that the importation of orchids involves not only a knowledge of the enormous number of species, their distribution, but a general ability to overcome the enormous number of difficulties that are encountered in this bureaucratic world of ours today. Having prepared the ground, and the necessary contacts, and success-fully obtained the imported orchids, one is still up against the greatest of all difficulties, namely that of acclimatising a plant to new and artificial conditions.

Before giving you a few details of the difficulties that arise this end in cultivating the newly imported plants. I must stress that in the whole world today there are scarcely half a dozen men who have experience of collecting orchid plants. I have mentioned two, but there are also three of four more expert American collectors who have met with considerable success. These collectors, however, go out for short periods of time and in most cases do not make the art of collecting orchids in the wild a life-time business. One is therefore, in the hands of a semi-permanent and often amateurish collector.

The majority of orchids that are imported into this country today are probably imported through agents in the various countries to which the orchids are native. These agents are naturally out to make a good living from the plants they re-forward to Europe. To obtain their best plants it is essential not only to make payments in advance of considerable sums of money, but to guarantee the heavy costs of air freight and duty.

In my own experience over the past four years I have estimated the cost of many specimen imported plants has doubled in the past decade. The plant when established and saleable is a very expensive proposition and few people are prepared to pay £20 for an imported orchid, although they will gladly part with £400—£500 for a drawing-room suite of three pieces of furniture!

The bread-and-butter plants such as *Odontoglossum pulchellum, Lycaste skinneri,* and several others are fairly easy to import in small quantities.

It is no wonder that the very great majority of commercial orchid growers in Europe concentrate on raising plants from seed. Even so, I think the intrinsic value of a genuine imported plant is worth all the trouble and costs of importation and establishment in our nurseries.

Such plants must be treated with great circumspection. I do not intend to go into great details, but there are certain essentials of cultivation which must be performed. If these imported plants arrive in perfect weather—which is not often the case—they may be laid out on wire trays in a heavily shaded position on the staging of an intermediate house with an average temperature of somewhere around 60° F. (15–16° C.). Sprayed daily once or twice with a very fine spray, these plants will probably be ready to pot up within two months.

If the plants are, however, shrivelled and in very poor condition, perhaps leafless, it is often necessary to dip them for 6–8 hours in a nutritive solution. Castor sugar is a useful basis for such a solution. If the plants are left too long in this solution, they will rot.

Generally speaking, a plant that is imported between April and June may be safely potted up at once even though there does not appear to be root action. Outside these months it is better to wait until root action begins, the plant being sustained by constant sprayings. In some cases it pays to stand the plant in a pot of fresh sphagnum moss, taking care not to allow the moss to be soaked, but rather to moisten it occasionally.

When an importation arrives it is essential to examine each plant very thoroughly, although all importations must be accompanied by a Certificate of Health and a Certificate of Origin; these Certificates can mean very little in fact unless it be a source of income to the issuing authorities and a source of satisfaction to the Civil Servants this side. Having ensured that the plants are free from disease and insect pests, it is still much safer to treat every plant with an insecticide before laying it on the wire trays of the benches. These trays are essential to allow the free circulation of air around the plant and prevent losses from damping-off.

One of the greatest difficulties associated with imported orchids is that of finding a suitable container in which to pot them, or basket them up. The man who collects the plants does not consider the man who is going eventually to pot the plants up! For example, a Laelia may grow all around the stem of a tree, and the rhizome will thus be curving in all directions and consequently bulbs facing in diametrically opposite directions. This makes potting well nigh impossible and only experience can teach you the best way to adapt each particular plant.

Having eliminated 10, 20, 30 and perhaps even 50 per cent of an importation during the course of their first six months in our greenhouses, there is, nevertheless, an enormous satisfaction in seeing the remaining fit plants putting out roots and perhaps establishing themselves firmly before the winter months set in. This is one step over, but there is still the problem of flowering the plant and finding the exact position in the nursery where it will best grow. Not infrequently, it is necessary to place a cool-house orchid in relatively warm conditions in order to establish it and before returning it to its normal, cooler, artificial growing conditions.

Better still, buy imported plants that have been established by well known growers. There are available today imported plants handled by dealers whose responsibility ends when you have paid for your importation (usually in advance) and who usually have no nursery let alone an address where you can call for advice. Many of my customers have experienced this perhaps financially attractive but often disastrous way of increasing their collections. The plant is literally a raw *jungle* plant and they often arrive at the latter end of the year when establishment is extremely difficult if not impossible. Once you have experience of growing imported orchids the risk is not too great and of course they cost less, as a rule, but by no means always, than the same plant bought from an established orchid nursery.

Before closing this introduction to the Appendices on the importation of orchids that follow, I would like to stress the point that it just does not pay an amateur to import orchids direct. Very rarely can an amateur with only a few years' experience succeed in saving even a large enough proportion of an importation to make it worth while from the financial point of view. It is rather like the man who moves his home and with it takes the established plants from his old garden and tries to re-establish them in his new garden. A mature plant will rarely be moved with impunity. Better to buy a new set of young and vigorous plants that can adapt themselves to their new conditions.

One of the early books on orchids is Millicent's *Adventures of an Orchid Hunter*. The very phrase 'Orchid Hunter' suggests to the sober-minded, a book with a modicum of information on orchids, and their collection in their native habitats. This Victorian novel was published in 1891. In 1930 another book appeared with the luxury title *The Odyssey of an Orchid Hunter* by Captain Burdett. In it appears in print, as far as I can remember, the name of one single orchid, *Vanda sanderiana,* known to the natives in the Philippines as the 'Walling-walling'. These books are typical of journalistic reports and, although readable, are most inaccurate.

Schomburgk's two volumes (in German) on British Guiana, were the subject of my reading some years ago when I was inflicted with a few days of virulent influenza and confined to bed. I chose this work because I thought I might glean information on some of the Guiana orchids. I was sadly disillusioned. Do not go to the bother of collecting or borrowing such amiable descriptions of amusing voyages unless your penchant is for travel books. Rather, if you want a background of orchid hunting with a fair trace of truth and reality, read the *Orchid Review* back to 1893, and do not on any account miss the younger, fresher and intensely detailed and graphic reports of our contemporary orchid hunters to be found in many numbers of the *American Orchid Society Bulletin,* and the German bulletin *Die Orchidee*—a Hamburg publication. I recommend them—thoroughly—as also *l'Orchidophile, The Orchid World,* and other genuine orchid classics. These articles are written by actual orchid collectors and not journalists.

In the *Orchid Hunter* by Millicent there are one or two noteworthy points made by the author, and Captain Burdett's book is good reading. At least this most intrepid traveller had the satisfaction of sending home some real live and fine specimens of *Vanda sanderana,* the 'Walling-walling' which means 'the beautiful'. I remember, as a boy, these plants—housed at our Bruges nurseries—and fanned day and night by electric fans which

circulated a near-ninety per cent humidity. They were introduced to Europe, thanks to a great friend of my late Uncle Fred,
an orchid amateur, and a very old member of the Royal
Horticultural Society's Orchid Committee, the late Mr Henry P.
Lawson, who financed the importation. One of them, a very fine
form indeed, and comparable to any of the contemporary
Hawaiian forms, was exhibited at the R.H.S. Show at Olympia
in 1937 and obtained an F.C.C. Well do I remember delivering
this plant to a mad amateur in the vicinity of the Manchester
aerodrome. The hunt for his home was little less exciting—I then
thought—than was that for the plant. Imagine my reaction
when, full of the romantic thoughts of that one plant's journey
across the Eastern Hemisphere, I saw it solemnly put on a *unique*
fourteenth-century refectory table, off which I supped, news-
paper for tablecloth, a little later on in the evening, on bread and
cheese, for indeed this amateur—like so many of us orchid
growers—was mad! Mad keen. A thousand pities that a bomb
should have ended that story.

A great pity perhaps the only *Vanda sanderana* (from the same
source) to have carried five live and lovely spikes of blooms in a
Welsh homestead in 1947 should also now be no more. This
plant went the way of other orchidaceous relatives, into a
bonfire, for the owner, near death would not allow it to survive
him. He loved his plants as much as he was little progeny
conscious. Another mad, but oh! so loving an amateur, for I
knew him well. So much for being side-tracked by Captain
Burdett.

In Millicent's book there is an interesting reference—one of the
few appertaining to orchids—to the fact that on an average he cut
down 10,000 trees to obtain 4,000 sound Odontoglossums. An
economic proposition those days, and one he justified quite
simply by stressing the acreage—or rather, square-mileage—of
native forest.

An interesting fact that is confirmed by all orchid hunters since
and before Millicent (my grandfather had a dozen collectors in
this area before that time) is the incredible 'mix-up' of warm and
cool growing orchids in a given small area. Near La Palma, a
village not far from one of the emerald mines which still survive,
were found *Odontoglossum crispums* galore (now quite extinct),
and down in the valleys and on the low hills around, *Cattleya*

warscewiczii, a lover of warmth. But even in those far off days of the nineties, Millicent writes of O. *crispum* 'the best were cleared away—*long ago*'. Again up on the hills the lovely *Miltonia phalaenopsis,* and down in the dales the warmth loving *Oncidium kramerianum.* All within the bounds of an area equal to that of our English Rutlandshire! Ocana in Santander then gave rich returns in O. *pescatorei,* 10 days' mule ride from the La Palma. Up to a few years ago you could only see seed-raised O. *pescatorei* at Charlesworth's in Sussex.

Bucaramanga is another word, less musical perhaps than La Palma, but one with force and meaning in the pre-1900 orchid history. It heads the letters of many hundreds of epistles in several languages from our Colombian travellers up to 1914. It brought to mind Medellin and Bogota—I imagine—an isolated comfortable hotel, probably wood-built, in a village-town of perhaps 2/3,000 souls in the 1890's. How welcome to these men of courage after months of trundling up and down mountains. Their extremes of comfort and endurance must have been akin to the contrast of *Masdevallia harryana,* small and pert at 8,500 ft in Andean hills not far away, and the showy magnificent Cattleyas *dowiana* and *warscewiczii* found lower down in the valleys; to the icy freshness of *Odontoglossum crispum*, and the lovely warmth of a blue butterfly. Such men were Arnold, Ernst, Klaboch, Kerbach, Perthuis (who also knew Peru well), Oversluys, Schmidtchen, and Wallis, to mention but a few of those who travelled for my grandfather under their great leader Forget— and loved it! I have before me, as I write these notes, a map of *those* days, in perfect condition though well travelled, the cloth perfect, the squares neatly cut, the folds untearable, but printed in Long Acre by Edward Stanford before the Queen (Victoria) had been reigning fifty years!

Other names of intrepid travellers commemorated by orchids and other plants are kept alive today. We have their correspondence written on note-sheets, hotel bills (and *how* revealing they are!) shipping bills and even bank-drafts. They include men like Abel, Bartholomans, Birchenall of Mexican fame; Chesterton, Darnel and Lehman of the West Indies; Wallis and Hennis of Panama and Costa Rica; Lingreen of Paraguay; Ortgies and Forget of Brazil (the latter explored almost *every* corner of Central America as well); Seidle of British Guiana; Humboldt of

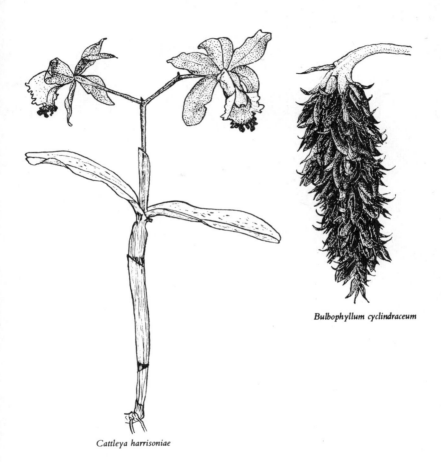

Cattleya harrisoniae

Bulbophyllum cyclindraceum

Madagascar; Lehmann of the Celebes and Indo-China; Ericcson of the Far East; to mention but some of the many who travelled for Sander in the pre-1914 days, when as many as twenty-three collectors were out orchid hunting at the same time, and not forgetting dear old W. Frost who died recently. He collected animals for the Regents Park Zoo (even more hazardous than collecting plants) at the tender age of seventy plus. Orchids were always a side-line with him, though properly financed—which he never was—he could have re-introduced all the rare species from Cochin-China and those parts of the Far East now lost to us through Communist penetration. But Frost has a successor.

There are today at least two young men from Europe who have made successful expeditions to South America. The first young man I would mention is Rupert Donovan, late of Clare College, Cambridge. I managed with the aid of one or two orchid growing customers to finance an expedition to British Guiana of which he was in charge. This expedition was in great part successful and one of Mr Donovan's most interesting letters I include in this book under Appendix B. I have followed this with my own account of a more recent expedition to Venezuela and Trinidad.

The other young man was a German, I must leave his name unwritten here and call him George. Now George has penetrated into many miles of jungle and savannah in the quest of species, some of which he has re-introduced. More of him we shall hear in the years to come, but the following extracts from his correspondence (1955) will show you that orchid hunting is not a thing of the past.

APPENDIX A

EXTRACTS FROM GEORGE'S LETTERS IN 1955

From Costa Rica (San Jose) in January 1955:

'Could it be due to the revolution here the (our) letter did not arrive . . . 125 *Miltonia endresii,* 100 *Warscewiczella discolor,* 40 *Masdevallia enthrochaea,* 45 *Masdevallia reichenbachiana* (alas! all those arrived dead due in great part to air-transport and stowage in unheated compartments) . . . sometimes it is hard travelling alone—carrying 80 pounds pack for 4–5 hours from a high rain forest in the clouds to the fizzling hot lowlands . . .'

A little later from the same address:

'*Epidendrum endresii* grows at about 2,000 metres on oak trees above swampy mountain bogs. It likes it cool but bright . . . also *Oncidium warscewiczii* a lovely yellow cloud-forest species (2,400 metres 60° F.) . . .'

From Panama City, February, 1955:

'. . . my visa expires the day after tomorrow . . . (not the least of a modern orchid hunter's troubles is the *incredible* red-tape, which incidentally does not end with the consignment in this country) . . . I have now just $180 to carry me into South America . . . I would be violently hurt if these shipments should be said to arrive in England decayed or frozen (they *did*) as I now have to see a doctor to cure me from an intestine disease which I have picked up while collecting *Cattleya dowiana*, not to mention a brand of jungle-mites to make me scratch the . . . : many of my plants look like divisions . . . *Lycaste skinneri* is exceptionally nasty this way—bulbs rot like nobody's business during the drying process, and only the absolute healthiest bulbs seem to survive . . .'

From Guayaquil, Ecuador, March, 1955:

'. . . I have some 280 very fine Odontoglossums from 1,500 metres altitude. They flower now carrying magnificent spikes (*O. hallii*) they receive rain and fog every afternoon with sunny warm mornings from January to May, a warm dry summer following . . .'

From Guayaquil a little later:

'According to the map the region in upper Riobamba where it (*Miltonia vexillaria*) must exist is completely uninhabited, with the next Indian settlements (fortunately no savages, though naked tribes not speaking Spanish) some 40 miles distant . . . risky to go into this country without guides . . . to talk about rarity of certain orchids, to collect the truly marvellous *Epidendrum schumannianum* (a *real* gem) in number, one had better be born a monkey . . . they grow on trees so high in the jungle so dense that solely spotting a plant is more than a headache . . . People nowadays, even in these countries, are greatly interested in orchids, and the consequent raiding of the forests year after year by the natives make them rather infrequent . . .'

From Guayaquil still later:

. . . I am now in the very unfortunate and difficult position of having torn my clothes and boots in the forests, so that from my last 50 sucres (about 3 dollars) 35 had to be spent for just getting my only pair of shoes repaired leaving me just enough to buy stamps for this card and but a final pack of cigarettes. I have just made the acquaintance of another orchid enthusiast, who has done enormous collecting here (Schumann I think), and for years. Through this gentleman, I now know localities for *Stanhopea grandiflora, Odontoglossum harryanum, Odont. crispum* and *pescatorei, Miltonia warscewiczii, Odont. hallii*, etc. ! ! . . . Besides, do you know that there is one way of getting the marvellous orchid, which carries your name and has not been collected since 1895, *Maxillaria sanderana*?!!!—The same district (the old one for *Max. sanderana* is now a banana-plantation) habitates a new, even more beautiful Maxillaria, not named yet. We talked and studied maps all night until 5 a.m. . . . I am just too eager to take part in this expedition into unmapped country . . . This country is a true paradise for orchids (I also know a stand of these long drooping-petalled Selenipedium!) however, almost unexplored. Enough to say, that I was offered shrunken heads by Jivaro-Indians in Quito . . . Aucas and cannibals too, live east of the Cordillera Oriental. Anyhow, I will risk my neck getting all these orchids out of pure fanaticism . . .'

From Cuenca, Ecuador, April, 1955:

'. . . These plants (Miltonias) originate from 9,000–10,000 ft altitude. It is very cold here, the forest is wet and mossy—plants grow there in moss and roots of polypodium ferns, the best ones, where they receive a bit of sunlight—however that is not why I write you. I know where to get *Odont. crispum*! This plant is rare and takes weeks to collect in quantity,—please immediately write (to Guayaquil) how many you want of it and at what price . . .'

From Guayaquil, May, 1955:

'. . . Between 1,200 and 1,500 metres altitude I found one of the most magnificent Maxillarias I have ever seen. These gorgeous Maxillarias with their numerous 4 in. flowers in pure white with only a mauve-striped lip terminating yellow (slightly fragrant) rival the white *Lycaste skinneri*! This is an extraordinarily rare orchid and one of the most dangerous to collect from the point of risking one's neck. They grow singularly in trees not under 75 ft high, which hang on the vertical walls of deep (300–500 ft) shady and gloomy canyons. Nearly constantly for 24 hours a day you will find fog or rain beating down here, although it is still bright like milk from the fog. Better cultivate it like you used to with *M. luteo-alba*, as you once wrote me. Because of the rarity, beauty and pains to collect it I would, for once, ask you a price of $5.00 on it, knowing you will be able to collect quite a profit on it. I am going to send you 100 plants, however doubt if I could supply another 100 if you would want more of it. Believe me, you will be absolutely delighted! (We were: *Maxillaria sanderiana*). Another orchid from about the same region is a huge Lycaste with 5–6 in., but green flowers and a brown lip. The bulbs are awfully heavy and I cut off whatever I could. I think I have about thirty plants for you . . .'

From Puyo/Napo Pastaza, Ecuador, June, 1955:

'The reason for writing you again is that I have run into quite an interesting district for orchids, so that I will soon be able to mail you another lot. Kindly apply for an import licence as soon as possible, as I have already some 110 *Huntleya Burtii* . . . On my way back to Guayaquil I will be stopping over in two more places of both *Cordillera oriental* and *occidental*, on one of which I have spotted *Brassia longissima* on my way east. The "roads" are

133

the worst on earth. The stretch down the Pastaza between Banos and Puyo is a hair-raising one. Down here, everything stops. To get the Huntleyas, I walked some 25 miles every day on Jivaro paths which are made of squeezed-out sugar cane and decayed logs. They usually stop after some 7 miles in the bush and then you "drown" in the swamp, which goes right up to one's hips. No fun collecting these Huntleyas, for sure! Also, it rains like mad every second hour and the mosquitoes are quite as much of a pest as the pit vipers and arboreal snakes. The real danger, though, is to get lost and walk into the Auca country or a Jivaro trap south of Canelos . . .'

APPENDIX B

Kamarang Mouth (B.G.)
August 14th, 1959

'Dear Mr Sander,

'The collecting trip that I outlined for you in my last letter from Paruima has proved a tremendous success, and, if all goes well, the plants should reach you within the next 3 weeks. All was not plain sailing, however, as you will hear.

'Paruima is an Amerindian mission station on the upper Kamarang, set on a large bend in the river from which the forest has been cleared. All around the mission is dense rain forest which is permeated by numerous boggy trails that connect the scattered Amerindian settlements in the area. The trail that I took lay alongside the rapids above the mission, and my two guides made little allowance for the fact that I was not used to walking in thick mud, and it wasn't long before I was severely out of breath. But we hadn't been walking for an hour before we came across a wide variety of orchids on the moss-covered trees that bordered the trail. At first there didn't seem to be anything very exciting until I suddenly became aware of a faint chocolate smell in the air—the more I tried to trace it, the more elusive it became. It was obviously a flower of some sort, and one of the guides, Albert, assured me it was an orchid which he had seen in flower on this part of the trail before. Then, quite suddenly, I smelt it again—a very powerful chocolate-vanilla smell and Albert asked "You smelling, sir?"; soon we found it—a magnificent plant of *Polycycnis vittata* with a spike of chocolate coloured flowers giving off a very powerful perfume. We also discovered some magnificent plants of *Coryanthes maculata, Peristeria guttata, Scuticaria steelii, Batemania colleyi, Epidendrum radicans, Mormodes buccinator* and *Gongora atropurpurea*—not to mention a host of miniatures, *Stelis* and *Pleurothallis* species, etc.: Obviously we couldn't carry these plants with us on the journey, so we fixed them to a large tree to wait for our return.

'As I told you in my last letter, any real quest was for *Cattleya lawrenceana* on the Guiana-Venezuelan border. The plant is an

135

inhabitant of the Venezuelan Grand Savannah—a 3,000 ft high plain that extends for hundreds of miles westwards into Venezuela. Paruima is about 1,500 ft so I was rather anxiously waiting the climb. I had made a serious mistake in carrying my hammock and clothes which, after a very short time seemed to weigh a ton—the Indians don't mind how much they carry, and presume that you carry what you are physically capable of carrying or what you don't trust them to carry—they would never dream that you were trying to do them a favour! However, after many hours of stumbling along a very muddy trail, crossing numerous streams that served to keep one's feet permanently damp, and tripping over endless roots, we reached the base of the escarpment that leads to the savannah. To my horror, the Indians walked that same speed up the hill as they had along the flat, and in next to no time I was retching with exhaustion an awfully long way behind. After much resting and stumbling on we reached the savannah at 4 o'clock.

'Quite suddenly the forest stopped, and there, stretching as far as the eye could see, was a grassy plain, across which blew a delicious cool zephyr bringing a short-lived relief from the dampness of the forest. I say short-lived because at this time of year the savannah is made almost uninhabitable by biting insects. In the day-time there is the caboura fly—about the size of a greenfly—which leaves an intensely itchy bite and which occurs in quite overwhelming numbers, and at night there are mosquitoes which are avoidable with netting and sandflies which are not. All in all, by the time my hopelessly inadequate three-quarter bottle of insect repellent had run out, life became increasingly irritating.

'We were three days reaching the creek where I was assured the orchids could be found. The journey was a memorable one, as it was my first contact with tropical rivers in flood. The first river I crossed with two sticks as supports and one Indian on either side to catch me if I slipped—the second river was about twice as deep and twice as fast flowing, so, my nerves being not quite at their best, I decided to swim, and let the Indians make two journeys for my gear. Unfortunately I didn't realise until it was too late that the banks of the rivers were lined with razor-grass, and my gentle bare-footed skipping along trying to find a launching site was very painfully rewarded, and one of the cuts I got is now septic and has caused my foot to swell up and make walking almost impossible.

'The savannah has a very rich ground orchid flora, but apart from many Catasetums and Sobralias I couldn't recognise any other genera. Nevertheless, I have collected a representative selection for you.

'The nights proved bitterly cold, and my entire wardrobe was often insufficient to keep out the chilling dampness of the night air. How the Indians ever managed to sleep with their thin, tattered clothes is still a mystery to me. Most nights, the three of us would all be squatting round the fire by about 4 o'clock in the morning, and it was in this homely atmosphere that I began to learn something of the Indian way of life and their opinions of the various Europeans and Guianese who visit them. There is no doubt that they regard all other peoples as physically weak— apart from a few outstanding exceptions such as the D.O. of the area—and that on the whole they are suspicious of black people. They are very trusting, however, and never ask for any advance payment if you hire them for a trip, although they have an ingenious trick of bringing all their friends along with them and expecting you to pay them as well. One outstanding virtue of the Indians is their simplicity—they can't hide their feelings and they usually say exactly what they think (possibly because their pidgin English doesn't give them much scope for nuance) which makes for very cordial relations as long as you all have the same end in view. I flattered myself that I was a great hit, until I discovered the real reason for their visit to the savannah in such awful weather—it was fish!

'The day before we reached "the creek", the Indians spent the morning weaving cane baskets for the orchids and also for the fish that they had come to collect. Game is very rare around the mission owing to the density of Indian population, and the river Kamarang is very poorly supplied with fish. I was rather surprised by the large size of their fish baskets and wondered whether they weren't being a little optimistic with such a short time and so little food between us all. But primitive fish like primitive people are not so wily as their educated brothers and a little worm on the end of a very obvious bent pin was attacked with remarkable vigour. I have never seen so many fish in such a small stream (about 3yds. across) and there wasn't one fish left after the Indians had been at it for an hour or so—their haul was colossal, and it wasn't until the fish were all being smoked that the Indians deigned to look for some orchids for me.

'From a long way off, the creek appeared as a green line across the dull monotony of the savannah, and when we got there I found that the trees on either side were much smaller and drier than those of the rain forest and extended for some twenty or so yards on each side of the stream. After searching for an hour or so, both the Indians came back with the rather astounding announcement: "No orchid", and looked at me as though to say:

' "It's getting late, don't you think we ought to go home?" to which I replied with one which said:

' "We're staying here all night if necessary until you find some orchids" and without further ado we all set off for another try.

'It was just after I had let off the most fabulous bout of bad language to express my feelings to the savannah for the flies, bogs, razor grass, etc., that I saw a miserable black orchid about 20 ft up the branch of an old tree. I yelled for the two Indians and after much scrambling and poking we got the plant down and imagine my delight when, after scraping of the fungus that was strangling it, I uncovered a very sick but genuine specimen of *Cattleya lawrenciana*. I can't tell you how exhilarating that moment was, when after months of planning and organising I had at last found the plant which had been the goal of the trip—suddenly the savannah seemed a wonderful, exciting place, full of fantastic orchids. Within an hour we collected fifty magnificent plants of *lawrenciana*, they seemed to be everywhere. But that wasn't all—we found *Epidendrum aromaticum*, which has the most exquisite perfume of all the orchids we found—and, most exciting of all, on an isolated tree we found an enormous bunch of Coryanthes in flower, and the flowers were pure white! The whole plant was a pale yellow, instead of the normal green, and there wasn't a speck of colour on the flowers or spike. Naturally I took a number of colour photos to convince you of this incredible find; although I searched the whole creek, I never found another plant of Coryanthes—so this could well be an isolated variant. For two days we collected vigorously, and discovered *Epidendrum crassilabium*, *Trichopilia fragrans*, *Rodriguezia secunda*, *Scaphyloglottis prolifera*, *Trigonidium obtusum*,

Hexadesmia sessilis and numerous others which I could not recognise.

'Keeping the plants proved very difficult, as it rained every night, and many of the plants rotted, but by building a special stage to put them on, we managed to keep the majority in excellent condition, waiting until the last possible moment before cutting off the back bulbs and packing up the plants for the long trek home to Paruima. By this time we were very short of food, and all our clothes were wet through, but what with the fish and the orchids we were all three very satisfied with the trip.

'The journey back was a nightmare. Nature was trying her hardest to make life impossible—the flies were everywhere, getting into eyes and nose, biting mercilessly on every square inch of exposed skin. Of course, it had to be Saturday sometime or other, and it happened on the way back. Paruima mission is a Seventh Day Adventist one, and on Saturday nobody does any work, so we spent a day with an Amerindian family in what

139

must be the most fly-ridden spot on the whole savannah sporting the fiercest sandflies I have ever encountered. Of course the two Indians spent the night in one of the houses while Joe Soap shared an exposed lean-to with the cattle. When I couldn't stand the cold any more, I laboriously set to work trying to light a fire—an art at which the Indians are remarkably adept, but which finds me at my most clumsy—nevertheless after many minutes and many matches I at last got a spurt of flame going and put some water on to boil . . . well, perhaps it was some sort of punishment for my bad language that just when the water was on the boil and everything was ready to make some tea, one of the logs supporting the billycan rolled over and all the water spilt into the fire neatly putting it out and robbing me of a desperately needed cup of tea!

'Soon we were on our way again, and with the help of one of the villagers got across the first river by canoe, but the second river was far too high to cross and we had to stop and wait for the water to go down, which it fortunately did over night. Meanwhile, the Indians took me to see the falls where this river, the Utchi, tumbles 720 ft into a steaming chasm in the heart of the rain forest. It was a magnificent sight as the swollen river hurled itself over the precipice with a deafening roar that echoed for miles down the forested valley. It was lucky that I didn't join it, for when we came to cross the river the current was terrific and half-way across I got stuck and couldn't move. While trying to change position, I came head on to the current and was relentlessly pushed over and bashed from rock to rock down the rapids. The Indians, who themselves were having the utmost difficulty crossing, were powerless to help and if it hadn't been for a well-placed overhanging branch things may have turned out very differently—as it was I was lucky to get away with a bruised knee and strained ankle.

'The journey down the Paruima seemed endless although it was all downhill. The paths were even wetter than before and we slipped everywhere, but at least our previous orchid collection had survived and I made arrangements to have them collected later that evening. By the time I got back I could hardly walk, and it was as much as I could do to stagger up to the mission and buy something to eat, because my food had run out 2 days ago and I'd been living on baby milk flavoured with tea!

140

'Next day I and the orchids spent 16 hours sitting in a very small dug-out canoe while the two Amerindians paddled us back to Kamarang where I hoped to catch a mid-monthly flight if there was one. It says a lot for the Amerindians that they can get things organised very quickly if you implore them hard enough, and that they will paddle a canoe for 16 hours virtually non-stop for the princely sum of 4 shillings. We left as soon as it was light with the river still covered by a diaphinous mist that made us shiver in its chill dampness. The canoe must have been the smallest in the village—there was a majestic 3 in. of freeboard and not an inch to stretch or alter position. Nature was at her most boring, as though, like the Indians, she too thought it was a stupid thing to hurry and wanted to try and show me the folly of my ways; not a bird, not a butterfly, nothing except the endless brown river getting imperceptibly wider as the day went on. The paddlers seemed to go slower and slower, the heat was unbearable as was the wretched position to which I had resigned my body for the journey. Dusk brought a strange relief, and as the shadows lengthened and the frogs began to croak, the river became alive with peculiar sounds; every little stream sounded like a waterfall, strange night birds wailed across the eerie blackness, shrieking parakeets shattered the calm, and gradually the air became colder. The front paddler turned and asked me for a torch as he was trying to find the entrance to a fast-flowing stream that cut off one of the bends in the river. The beam of the torch was like a formless disc on the forest wall, too pale to reveal any colour and too small to give anything a recognisable shape.

'Then, suddenly, we were in the rapids, rushing frantically along; the Indians having lost control of the canoe were yelling and screaming at each other, desperately trying to dodge the huge rocks round which the canoe was whisked by the racing water. Straight ahead the torch beam picked out a huge tree that had fallen across river and in an instant the canoe was thrown sideways against it and lurched over to one side. As the water poured in, we forced the canoe away from the tree and immediately were hurled back into the mainstream and out into the inky river once more. We had passed through the short cut in 15 seconds.

'So much for the quest for *Cattleya lawrenceana*— fifty plants in good shape waiting for the next plane to take them to Georgetown and then to you, plus, of course a great variety of other plants which I know you will be interested in having. My next collecting trip is to the Rupununi savannah to get you *Cattleya superba* which you requested, and after that a trip to the coastal rivers to get you *Oncidium lanceanum*, more Coryanthes, more Scuticaria, etc.:

'I'll be writing in a fortnight or so when I've finished the next trip—till then, all the best.

Yours,
Rupert.'

APPENDIX C

COLLECTING ORCHIDS IN VENEZUELA
BY THE AUTHOR

After a not unpleasant trip of 15 hours from Los Angeles Airport, cramped in the usual Pan-Am bus style, but broken by a stop off at Guatamala city, my friend 'Wiggs' Williams and I were pleased to alight at Caracas Airport. We were delighted to find that 'Stalky' and Nora Dunsterville were at the Airport to meet us in the middle of the night. 'Stalky', who is known by this nickname, as his father was the original 'Stalky' of Stalky & Co. (Rudyard Kipling), has recently retired as managing director of Esso, the largest oil company in the world. He is also the government-appointed geographical surveyor and is known for his many explorations in Guyana. The lovely national stamps of Venezuela were designed by him.

It was swelteringly hot. The drive through the wonderful modern city of Caracas was exciting but the sight of the entrance to his most beautiful home, some 10 miles out of town up in the hills, was a great relief, for we were very tired.

The next morning through the variable-pitch formica window blinds I could not only feel the softness of the breeze but could see the morning mist over the hills beyond the dewy grass lawn surrounded by Bougainvilleas of many colours. I watched a small humming bird taking its breakfast from the Bougainvillea nearest to my window—a lovely sight.

We left Caracas at lunch time and had an interesting 300-kilometre drive to a little port on the South Atlantic called Puerto La Cruz, where we stayed overnight. On the way there we saw a number of Orchids, and an enormous quantity of Bromelliads. This road lies between the coastal road and the forest of Guatapo. From either side of the road there is dense tropical growth of great beauty. Banana plantations predominate in the areas near the small towns. Lianas and *Vanilla pompona* entwine the huge trees. In the area are many Orchid species *Sobralia (violacea?)* *Schomburgkia humboldtii*—of which we saw one in flower subsequently on a huge mango—*Scaphyglottis*—a very persistent weed!— and Gongoras galore. Maxillarias, a *Rodriguezia, Lycaste (macrophylla?) Cochleanthes* and Epidendrums are also to be found here and of course the ubiquitous *Epid. nocturnum.* Also Catasetums *Vanilla (penicilata)* and *Oncidium sphacelatum.*

The drive to the Orinoco through the savannah scrub to El Tigre and thence through the Llanos to the capital of Ciudad Bolivar proved uneventful. The best coffee I have ever tasted in my life was here at El Tigre, the Esso centre; at last I could see just a faint justification for that (to me) irksome slogan, 'Tiger in your Tank!' There were unattended booths on the roadside in the savannah with *Cattleya violacea* for sale. If one stopped, a seller would turn up from nowhere—in one minute flat! We crossed the great Orinoco into Cuidad Bolivar, where we stayed in the only air-conditioned hotel.

Cuidad Bolivar! The Orinoco! Magic words! Many times have I heard and read about this capital, the headquarters and rest centre for my grandfather's travellers after months of tracking or mule packing. The river, still very broad here, with its many tributaries and rapids, was known almost yard by yard to Grandfather's men (see *Sander, The Orchid King* by A. Swinson, Hodder and Stoughton, 1969). From our breakfast table next morning we could see porpoises sporting in the river, and yet that must have been well over a thousand miles from the estuary.

Soon after breakfast we were driven by friends of Stalky to the airport, where he had laid on a private plane—A Cessna four-seater (we were five up with the pilot. The Canaima landing strip is only a few hundred yards from the rest camp. The site is glorious and bathing is possible in a lagoon below the Falls.

Around Canaima and on the banks of the Carrao we found *Bifrenaria minuta* and *aurantiaca*, *Brassavola martiana*, *Batemannia colleyii*, *Aganisia sp.* (first described in the Botanical Register in 1839), probably *pulchella*, *Aspasia variegata*, *Otostylis lepida* and other species.

Orchid Island (Rio Carrao). Just up river from Cananima about an hour's journey in the 8-metre dug-out the river splits into two to form Orchid Island. Not many decades ago this was filled with Orchids. Now, the trees are pretty well bare of plants. As we left the sandy beach for this mini-jungle and literally only two or three yards in from the shore, we actually found an Orchid! It proved to be an *Aganisia*, probably *A. pulchella*. We walked the length of the island before returning to the boat and continuing our journey upstream.

Tepuis are sandstone table mountains which come almost vertically out of the Guayana. The main forests around them are rich in Orchids. The first sight of this magnificent mountain rock I shall never forget. Some 7,000 feet high, this particular Tepui has on its northern face the magnificent Angel Falls. These in wet weather fall a sheer 3,800 feet to end up in broken spray so fine as to appear to be mist in the cavernous forested bottom pool. The first man to land there was Angel who landed in his plane on a bog and was unable to take off. He managed somehow to descend safely on foot to the plateau below. Only two expeditions have succeeded in climbing this Table Mountain and the first one was led by Stalky. It turned out that the terrain, although intensely interesting, was not rich in Orchids.

The Ahonda Valley. Biting into the Auyantepui a little down river from the Angel Falls is a short valley and river known as The Ahonda and never previously explored. This was our main objective. Imagine our disappointment when we found that there was not sufficient water in the river to take the canoe up. It did not matter much, for walking either on the river bed or the huge granite rocks or just inside the forest proved most exciting and interesting and fairly fruitful in plants. It is strange how light and bright it is one foot down from the banks flanking the jungle and how different the whole feeling and climate is just *inside* the jungle where once more than ten feet from the river and the reflected light through the interstices of the branches, one can very easily get lost. We all had machetes to assist in making the path for our return journey easier. We found a number of epiphytes including Epidendrums, Aganisias, a Catasetum and what were probably Oncidiums on a huge boulder in the middle of the river, a boulder which had originated many decades ago from the top of the Tepui which now loomed almost vertically above us.

Drosera anglica. Perhaps the highlight of this exploratory trip up the Ahonda Valley was to me the discovery of a sundew and not the many Orchids. I found a large clump of it clinging to the edge of a bank thriving I should say in full sun some 10 to 12 hours per day and of a brilliant reddish colouring. I managed to bring back home in my sponge bag a large clump of it which survived for some time, but did not like my greenhouses. I thought it strange to find *Drosera anglica* in a tropical country, but apparently it is distributed in many parts of the world, although, of course, not previously recorded in the Guayana.

145

M

The route taken by the author in Eastern Venezuela, indicated by a dotted line.

Downstream. The eve of our return to the camp at Canaima we came downstream in the twilight dark and camped on the left bank of a beautiful sandy beach. Part of the beach was covered with large pebbles and in my life I have never heard such an enormous noise as was made by the miniature frogs which, however, I could never see, for they were beneath the pebbles. Even my torch failed to reveal them. The only noise I have ever heard so intensely loud was that of the czicadas south of El Tigre the sound of which one could hear clearly in the car above the whirl of the engine. Our supper that night was cooked on a stove on stilts. The wooden stilts and base of the fire being covered with flat stones. We had a terrific thunderstorm but this fire under the waterproof shelter was not put out. Our light attracted a visitor who did not, however, stay to supper. He was bound for the diamond panning area of the Carrao River some 60 kilometres upstream.

Eventually we reached the airstrip, and were flown back to Cuidad Bolivar where we had a wonderful reception. Then we had a fast drive across the plain to El Tigre, where we stayed the night, and reorganised our packing for the next day's fast journey to the coast to Maturin and thence by air to Trinidad. The half-hour's flight to Port of Spain is a beautiful one and one has the island and the mainland in view at the same time. The airport at Port of Spain was quite the loveliest small and tidiest airport I have seen. It was strange to be driving on the left again. One felt very much at home after the wilds of Venezuela.

Our host, George Black, one of the keenest amateur Orchid growers I know, has his home sited many hundred feet above the port. From his garden one can look across the Bay and in the distance see the mainland and mountains of Venezuela. An unforgettable scene in daylight and even more beautiful as the sun sets. A few hours later we were to enjoy the beauty of the lights of this very English town spread out below us and listen to the sound of calypso bands and voices which came clearly up to George's hideout.

I was struck by the lack of advertisements and also by the strange sound—to me, new—of the steel limbo bands. The air was fresh and yet sweetly warm. Right in front of me as I looked out I could see the Southern Cross.

This delightful garden includes many hundreds of species and hybrids of orchids which we were to see in the morning in their full glory. Many of the hybrids were new crosses made by George Black himself and include such strange crosses as a *Cymbidium* with a *Grammatophyllum* which has already flowered, and an *Ansellia* from Africa with a *Cymbidium* from Queensland, another miraculous cross he has actually flowered.

The town, which we went through on our way out to the southern part of the island to search for Orchids, is extremely lovely. The first trip to the south brought us to the magnificent forests of Rio Caro. The first 15 miles were fairly well cultivated but beyond that the forests opened up in its natural state and yet the road we used, although narrow, was excellently metalled. The sugar plantations and small plots of vegetables had given way within 20 miles to the full forest. The houses along the roads were now considerably dispersed and attractive to look at, if small. They showed a certain prosperity and the children about exuded happiness and goodwill. Some 40 miles out the dwellings were mainly small shacks, and even here we came across the large oil pipe lines: one of the oldest oilfields in the southern hemisphere. It was strange to see the booster pumps right in the thick of the forest, like so many weird monsters, many of them dating back 40 years and still methodically pushing the oil down to the port and waiting tankers. It was strange to think that the trees here which were huge and generally in perfect condition should be in such contrast to the poor trees of the much burnt out forests of Venezuela which we had so recently been through. Many of these trees carried Orchids and I will list a few.

The most notable species we found in Trinidad was a patch of the now very rare *Paphinia cristata*. I had the pleasure of finding these few plants still growing on a felled tree in one of the last remaining patches of a few acres of the original forest in the central plain. This has by now been totally destroyed to provide small holdings of from 2 to 4 acres for the unemployed natives to farm. As the subsoil is heavy clay, there is virtually no means of ever making the soil fertile—unless it be for pig and poultry runs. It is to my friend, George Black, that the Island Administration owes the breeding of a tropical pig, a short life's work which together with Orchid growing were George's two hobbies. Other Orchids found were *Oncidium papilio, Xylobium, Cyrtopodium parviflorum, Dichaea, Coryanthes, Aspasia, Vanilla inod-*

148

ora, Stanhopea eburnea, Epidendrum nocturnum, E. atropurpureum, and *ferrugineum, Notylia, Pleurothallis* and *Lockhartia.*

One of the most inconvenient and painful obstructions in this forest was the 'Prickma' Palm. Our friend, Wiggs, most unfortunately slipped down a gulley and slithered along a 'Prickma' Palm which proved most painful. It took days before poor Wiggs got rid of his last spine and he must have had 30 or 40 of them in his body. One of the best sights I have seen was Gees, one of Mr. Black's native employees, scrambling up the trees for Orchids. Back at home later that evening we were given the most glorious dinner á l'Anglais and we appreciated the reason why George married his wife! The girls who served us were first-class and loyal members of the household—and they certainly knew how to cook.

The next day we went to the northern end of the island and climbed the tallest mountain in the island, Mt. Arupa. Here in these forests we found innumerable Orchids, including the lovely *Oncidium papilio* growing on fiddle trees. Here the Orchids are not limited to the trees but there are a number growing in the savannas below, in particular *Otostylis lepida*, a lily-like Orchid which was, unfortunately, not in flower. This plant is subject to a lot of swamping and very difficult to grow under cultivation as I have found out.

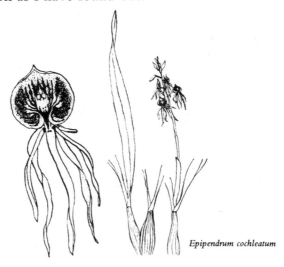

Epipendrum cochleatum

149

Back again in George's lovely home, evening drinks, a shower and change for dinner, where we met a considerable number of George's friends, nearly all of them interested in plants and in some cases Orchids—a real gardening crowd! And what can compare?

And now the sad last journey to the airport and a plane back to Heathrow. I wondered as we drove along in a heat of about 90° what the temperature would be like in London on the day of my arrival, May 1st. It turned out to be the hottest day of the year in London!

APPENDIX D

Much of the history of orchids lies around the life history of the late H. F. C. Sander, the founder of Sanders.

It has been my ambition for twenty years to make use of the many thousands of travellers' letters the contents of which divulge the history of the importation of orchids in my Grandfather's time. With this in view at last I found an excellent and well known author and B.B.C. producer—Arthur Swinson of St Albans whom I have known since our youth to write it under the title of *Sander the Orchid King*. For those interested in a very short resumé of the Sander firm now well over a hundred years old, the following will be of interest.

It was Mr Sander's intention to develop a seed business and, as a matter of fact, he did commence with a seed establishment in St Albans, working it up to a business of considerable size, producing amongst many fine strains the still popular *Nicotiana sanderiana*, the white Marguerite, Mrs F. Sander, and many other annuals. While working in Carter's nursery at Forest Hill he met Benedict Roezl, a lone orchid collector with but one arm.

In spite of this handicap, Roezl, a Bavarian, was a man of immense resolution and courage, yet had the faculty of engaging the trust of all native tribes he met. He it was who apparently first got Mr Sander interested in orchids. For years he had been sending home consignments, but had met with little monetary success, just sufficient to enable him to return for more. With Mr Sander's collaboration better prices were obtained; Roezl was able to retire and Mr Sander simply threw the seed business away, devoting the whole of his time to orchids.

A huge seed warehouse on the premises he first occupied in George Street, St Albans, was constantly filled to repletion, so much so that it was said you could not enter the room without treading on orchids. Later, however, he built a private house and a huge nursery of some 4½ acres covered with glass in the Camp district of St Albans, the name 'Camp' being derived from the fact that Julius Caesar is said to have camped outside St Albans, then known as Verulamium.

With more space at his command, he engaged numerous collectors, but received perhaps the greatest help from information passed on by Roezl to Roezl's two nephews. An old import book dated 1886 gives some idea of the quantity of orchids received. In February entries were made of nineteen cases of Cattleyas from Wells, seven from Jochs, fourteen from Robelen, three from Foestermann, etc.

In March of the same year some 300 cases were received: From Brazil, Central America, Africa, Mexico, Guatemala, and so on.

Little can be said in one chapter of the adventures and hardships of these Sander collectors. Bartholomaeus, Klaboch, Kerbach, Hubsch, Kramer, Robelen, Humblot, Ericsson, Micholitz, Forget, Starker, Arnold and others were all trained men, whose object was to procure the orchids they were sent after, and if possible to find other new species.

Kerbach, who travelled largely in Central America, Bogota, etc., came home in the mid-nineties so infected with malaria that recovery was hopeless.

Arnold's end was uncertain, or at least as to the method by which he came by it. His body was found in an open boat on a branch of the Orinoco.

Ericsson was largely employed in the Far East, and was one of the few who did give some idea of the hardships encountered in searching for orchids. He was after *Coelogyne pandurata* and sent home a magnificent lot of plants which on arrival were all dead. When written to, his reply was that he wished people at home could realise what procuring and searching for other orchids meant. He declared he had been wading up to his waist in thick mud in terrible heat after this and other plants.

Eventually the collecting was left largely in the hands of two collectors, Micholitz in the Far East, Forget in the West. Both were tried men. Micholitz, like Roezl, was a Bavarian; Forget was a Breton. Engaged while quite young, they quickly proved their ability. They engaged sub-collectors and natives as required.

The beautiful *Dendrobium phalaenopsis* var. *schroderianum*, though known, was collected by Micholitz and an interesting record stands of his first consignment. It must be understood that although orchids are said to come from New Guinea, Borneo, Philippines, etc., too often their habitats are confined to small islands, for which local craft have to be engaged, or taken advantage of, and the plants when and if collected trans-shipped at Singapore. Micholitz had a haul of this wonderful species. It had never yet reached Europe in quantity and these were particularly fine plants, but the local boat caught fire. The cargo was entirely burnt. Micholitz cabled the sad news home, but Mr Sander's laconic reply was 'Go back, get more', and so came to hand the second lot of *D. phalaenopsis schroderianum*, which made that wonderful orchid procurable by all.

Micholitz's visits among the Papuans were always looked forward to with interest at St Albans. Though supposedly fierce and treacherous, Micholitz had gained their respect and in turn they had gained his. Their small tribal wars proved greatly advantageous to him. It was the custom in those days when a tribe went to war that the victors on their return should bring with them any brightly coloured foliage or flowering plants they might see on their return journey. *Acalypha sanderiana* is due to this native trait.

Perhaps, however, the greatest monument to his memory is *Cymbidium sanderi*, botanically known as *C. insigne*. Rumour of this fine species had reached Europe from Annam and Mr Sander decided to send Micholitz to that country about the year 1900. Little was known of the natives or of the flora and Micholitz's journey was a great success. *Cymbidium sanderi, parishii* var. *sanderi, erythrostylum, schroderi, cooperi, mavis* and *roseum* were discovered. The last three mentioned are not recorded as species. Doubt has been expressed as to their hybridity. A few plants of each were sent home, but later expeditions have failed to discover any more: perhaps they were natural hybrids.

C. sanderi, however, under which name the plant was certificated, has really made a revolution in the Cymbidium genus. The influence of its distinct stately habit and lovely flowers is present in practically every Cymbidium hybrid of today, and no genus is more largely grown for decorative purposes, the culture extending now to Africa, Australia and America.

Apart from the Cymbidium, he found a most remarkable Arachnanthe now lost to cultivation, two new Coelogynes, *C. lawrenciana* and *C. mooreana*, all of market value in horticulture today. A second journey, taken from a different angle, was not

153

so successful. Another plant for which he was sent, *Cymbidium parishii sanderii*, apparently hardly existed on this second track. Since Micholitz's retirement and death other efforts have been made to get this orchid, but with little success, only a few plants being collected.

Forget travelled chiefly in the west and was instrumental in sending home huge consignments of *Cattleya labiata, mendelii, schroderae, harrisoniae* and other showy plants. He re-collected *Laelia gouldiana* of which but one plant was known in cultivation, and *Laelia jongheana* of which but one plant was known in Europe. A strenuous worker, nothing was ever heard of his troubles and trials, but he collected the plants. Of an excitable nature, his death was due largely to excitement caused by his enthusiasm in the Great War. He arrived home periodically at intervals of 2 years, and it must be said that his health seemed in no way affected by the different climates in which he had lived.

In 1902 one consignment alone of twenty-eight cases contained 3,000 plants of *Cattleya labiata*. Apart from employed collectors, correspondents and agents were in communication with Mr Sander from practically all the tropical and sub-tropical countries. From Java, Ceylon, India, Singapore, Africa, Australia, they wrote when new plants or interesting orchids had been discovered, and there are few countries which have not yielded their quota of orchid species and new plants of other families to the firm of Sanders.

A railway siding was established on the nursery which abutted on the Great Northern Railway, and orchids used to arrive there at all times of the day and night, and at all periods of the year. In cold weather special efforts were made to keep them warm in the trucks and get them in the houses as soon as possible. Although the Importing Shed in which they were placed had a central and two side stages, it is recorded as having been so full from one of these consignments arriving in the night that in the hurry to unload the shed was over filled and the next morning several cases had to be lowered in the lift to the floor below to allow room for the cases to be sorted.

Some Other Orchid Collectors

Joe Birchenall, collector for Sanders during the years 1880–1900, collected in Central America and exported quite a number of orchids to Sanders until the unhappy day when he, like one or two other collectors, such as Pauwels and Ericcson, preferred to 'go native', and sent no more plants home. He is commemorated in a couple of quite insignificant species such as *Pleurothallis birchenallii*, but I cannot recall any outstanding orchid named after him. Some time after he deserted Sanders, he sent some plants home to England and himself returned. These plants were Central American and included many fairly good plants of *Lycaste skinneri*. At the time of his return, Charles Conningsby, one of Sanders' most outstanding foremen, and the father of the loyal and excellent orchid grower, Arthur Conningsby (an octogenarian, who was a personal friend of mine), had at that time retired to a small business in Dagnall Street, St Albans. Birchenall persuaded him to go out for a week with samples of the plants he had sent home. At the end of a tiring week, he decided to go into Church End (Bristol) where was the renowned collection of the late Mr Hamilton Smith, under the able hands of Mr Arthur Conningsby. Mr Hamilton Smith was not in the least interested in Lycastes at the time, his main interest lying in the first Cymbidium hybrids. After a short conversation, Mr Hamilton Smith very sportingly said: 'I will save you the bother of taking those samples home to St Albans. Leave them here.' In those days the price of Lycastes was roughly 1 shilling a bulb, and my guess is that the whole lot cost Mr Hamilton Smith less than a couple of pounds.

Now in due course one of these Lycastes flowered, and so large and beautiful and deep pink was the flower that Arthur Conningsby pointed it out to his employer, who showed, however, very little interest in this truly beautiful flower. He agreed, however, for the plant to be put up before the Orchid Committee of the Royal Horticultural Society in the Old Hall, Vincent Square. Carrying three fine flowers, this plant did not receive an Award, to the disappointment and surprise of Arthur Conningsby.

One year later the same plant produced nine flowers, and they were so large that they had to be staked far apart and with great difficulty, in order to prevent the flowers touching. Again, Mr Conningsby persuaded Mr Hamilton Smith to show the plant with a varietal name, 'Mrs Hamilton Smith'. Again, even with nine flowers, the Orchid Committee turned this very beautiful orchid down. Meanwhile, Mr Conningsby had discovered that by severing the leading bulb, he could obtain propagations very quickly, and by the end of the third year there were no less than twelve magnificent plants, each carrying numerous buds, and an ideal subject for an exhibit. Arthur felt sure that by exhibiting the dozen plants carrying between them over a hundred flowers, he was bound to get an F.C.C. Unfortunately, destiny decided otherwise.

About this time Mr Hamilton Smith's senior partner, Mr Mann, an elderly gentleman who was ill, saw the plants and expressed his desire to acquire them, and Mr Hamilton Smith, with perhaps an ulterior motive in his mind, sold the whole stock for £50. If we value this ulterior motive at another £50, we still have the stock sold for but £100, a figure which in those days was frequently paid for a single bulb and growth of a good imported orchid.

Now destiny had not finished playing 'ducks and drakes' with this most exquisite orchid—*Lycaste skinneri* var. 'Mrs Hamilton Smith'. Within a month Mr Mann had died. Mr Cooper, one of Sander's most knowledgeable salesmen and plantsmen, acquired that stock from Mr Mann's executors in less than no time, and the following factual report reflects strangely on the then Orchid Committee!

Mr Cooper, who considered this one of his best 'snips' of the year, sold the individual plants all over the country, and amongst the people who acquired them, was the late Sir Jeremiah Coleman. At the time of the sale, about 1916, the Manchester and North of England Awards were very serious affairs, and this lovely orchid obtained a first-class certificate and the Prima Award for the show held at Manchester. A little later the R.H.S. Orchid Committee gave the same plant an Award of Merit. Still later, Mr Perfect, the well-known and excellent grower to the late Sir Jeremiah Coleman, exhibited the same plant with only three flowers and obtained a first-class certificate at the Royal Horticultural Society! Subsequently the orchid obtained Prima Awards at the Ghent Floralies for the finest and most outstanding species of the whole show, this in 1928, if I remember rightly, and later still the Prima Award for the finest orchid in the Orléans show in the U.S.A.

This little story reminds me of another orchid of much more

recent date, a certain Paphiopedilum Lady Clunas (in fact to date the finest progeny of that most charming and relatively new species, *Paphiopedilum delenatii*), which only came into its own (after much lobbying) in the late fifties with a First-Class Certificate.

Johnny Pauwels was another product of the Sander School who did well. During his apprenticeship at Sanders he worked with Moffat in the old Printers' Shop, painting orchids. It is strange that a man with such artistic tendencies should eventually be chosen by the late H. F. C. Sander to travel for the firm, and, then, in a rather circuitous manner start up a business of his own in Belgium.

Ericson, a Swede, who collected for Sanders, is perhaps best known for his introduction of *Bulbophyllum ericsonii*, the 'Cup and Saucer' orchid. A consignment of *Coelogyne pandurata* sent by him with bulbs 5 in. high unfortunately opened up dead on arrival.

*   *   *   *

You will readily gather from the above extracts that orchid collecting today has increased rather than diminished in its hazards. This is due very nearly entirely to the incredible amount of bureaucracy. One great disadvantage is the necessity for permits to even enter a country, let alone collect plants. Another is the difficulty of getting plants to airports or ships. In the old days a mule cost little, and most navigable rivers boasted a weekly service either way, and which was reliable if slow. Life was more reasoned and plants could be prepared (dried and conditioned) for as much as 6 weeks travel over land and river to a port such as Barranquilla, whence to Colon and Europe in a matter of 3 weeks. Now, not only are the costs exorbitant, but the delay in conveyance from forest to nursery, increased rather than reduced by air transport, due to the well-nigh impossibility of obtaining the exact details of weight, numbers and varieties of a consignment (known only to the collector perhaps 500 miles from the coast) the certificates of health (whatever that means!) the export and import licences, and other factors which, to be perfectly correlated with the importer at his end, would necessitate a combination of luck and brain and a capacity for guessing beyond the powers of an average horticulturist lacking in departmental civil service training—or a radio transceiver! On

157

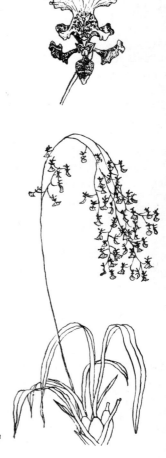

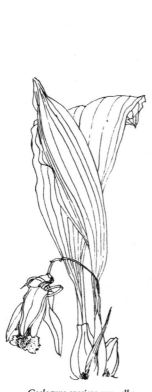

Coelogyne speciosa var. *alba*

Oncidium montana

top of this an aircraft flies at such a height, and prevailing conditions at intermediary airports, are such that plants often sweat or freeze alternately in quick succession. This and the huge freight rates (a good six-bulbed plant of *Laelia autumnalis* may cost from 12 to 18 shillings in air freight alone) practically kill importations, and can allow of no profit to the importer if the plants are to be sold at a competitive price. But the fun and thrill of collecting an importation of orchids will always remain. There is also the reward of an odd fine importation, when over half the plants survive, and within a year or two individual plants look once more like the real and beautiful creations they were in their pristine surrounds.

One regulation (Brazil) enforces the removal of *all roots*! This, from the *exporters'* point of view, sounds remarkably like imbecility to me, and yet I have no doubt certain South American civil servants could explain that away. How they could establish such a plant economically, let alone pot it up, they might be less successful in demonstrating. I could show you 200 Cattleyas, so treated and which wilted in our nursery, and much dead matter we still had to pay duty on this end in order to obtain the odd living remains.

Alas! for the sorry tale, but it does make for greater appreciation of a genuine established species when found in cultivation outside its normal habitat.

To conclude these few notes, may I suggest that you reverence a good plant of the God-made type when you get it, and propagate it well, and throw no bulb with a live eye away? It is worth its weight in sweat and worry, if not in gold.

16

Greenhouse Construction and Automation

~~~~~~~~~~~~~~~~~~~~~~~~~~~~~~

SPECIAL HOUSES are by no means necessary for orchid culture, but, to regulate the air and retain a moist atmosphere, alterations to an existing house may be necessary. A small ideal house for orchids in general would have its walls of bricks which should rise 4 ft from the ground, the roof anti-drip rafters should fall on to a plate resting on the walls. The side stages of 1 or 1½-in. square wood strips should be placed 3 ft from the ground level and should be 3 ft 6 in. in width with a 2 ft 6 in. path in between. The hot water pipes are placed at least 9 in. above the ground level, and above them about 12–15 in. below the slat stage is fixed a dummy stage on which is placed shingle, broken coke or similar moisture retaining material. The dummy stage should be of sufficient width as to prevent direct heat from the pipes impinging on the plants. The ridge board of the house should be about 8 or 9 ft from the ground level; a path may be made of wooden duck-boards or flat stones, but as much surface soil should remain as possible. Top ventilators, each some 2 ft long by 15 in. deep should be placed alternately a yard or so apart, or a patent ridge ventilator the whole length of the house may be installed (see page 150). Similar but narrower ventilators of wood should be constructed in the walls, so placed that when open the air passes near or around the hot water pipes. Side ventilators to open just above the level of the stages are better entirely dispensed with. If the house is isolated, the one end can consist of bricks. The measurements given are only approximate. Where side glass is in position it will often be found an advantage to have protective curtains of thick sacking or similar material so arranged that they can be drawn over the glass in very cold or sunny weather. Alternatively exterior wooden lath blinds may be used.

If possible, houses should be built running south-west or nearly so.

See plan on page 150 for an ideal layout for a small orchid house.

A small excellent teak or hard wood house complete with lathe staging and ventilators and adjacent contiguous potting shed may now be bought quite inexpensively and many are to be seen at the Chelsea Flower Show. An ideal two-sectioned standard 20 by 12 ft house need no longer cost a fortune and we shall be glad to advise you should you not have access to a good local horticultural builder.

In the past few years there has been a considerable amount of competition in greenhouse building. There are a number of very 'cheap' greenhouses of which I have some experience and which are indeed anything but inexpensive in the long run. It is no good building a house with ¾ × 1¼ in. straight rafters, the space between these rafters being over 20 or more inches. The glass will work loose under wind pressures. These houses are *too light*. True, they admit a lot of light, but they are not of sufficient

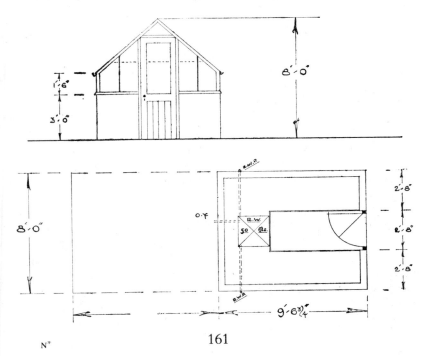

strength to last and resist even English climatic conditions. I do not hesitate now to recommend the well known major greenhouse builders, if you can afford them, but usually they are so fully booked with orders that they cannot execute an order within a reasonable period of time. On the other hand, there are one or two builders who specialise in orchid houses. One such person who has given complete satisfaction to many of my newer amateur customers is Mr. C. H. Whitehouse of Buckhurst Works, Frant, Sussex. He really does make a lovely job of a small house, which house can be extended to include the usual cool and intermediate divisions. Another first-class firm is that of Strawsons of Horley, Surrey.

There exist in North America orchid houses which have been so equipped as to be fully automatic. One of the most charming of genuine amateur growers in the State of Ohio has such a house. He is a personal friend of mine and frequently travels in Europe and other parts of the world, being absent as long as 6–8 weeks at a spell. His particular house is divided not as usually in this country in sections along the length of the house, but is divided vertically from the apex down to where normally would be found the central path. The air circulates automatically right round the two sections, the one side being preceded by a refrigerator in the end wall, and the other by a heater. Compensation for the heat is given by automatic water vapourisers and everything is worked to clockwork on highly sensitive thermostats and hydrostats and leaf-foils which activate the blinds. Even then there is the awful snag of snow which can only be remedied by a double roof which entails over shading.

To be more practical, I do recommend the introduction of one or two automatic factors. The automatic fan I have dealt with in Chapter 3. Automation in heating is almost invariably dependent on the supply of electricity. If the supply of electricity is not reliable or guaranteed, I do *not* recommend electric heating as a main source for greenhouses. If, however, it is used, then it is almost essential that some system be used which allows for a body of hot water to be raised to a high temperature, which therefore takes some time to cool down, giving heat out all the time. If electric heating is used, there should be a standby of paraffin. Many of the newer paraffin heaters are really odourless, although rather expensive. Automation in heating as I see it really depends on a boiler whether hand or screw fed, or better still gravity fed, which does the bulk of the work. Where electricity comes in so useful is to take over extra loads when outside conditions strain the boiler excessively, for example, in the warm division where a supplementary strip heater on the ledge of the glass can be very helpful. It must, of course, be combined with a thermostat which brings it into action only when the temperature of the greenhouse raised by the boiler drops below the desired figure. There are, by the way, few, if any, thermostats which are accurate to a degree or two. One has to allow for a range of as much as 7° F. (4° C.) in even the more expensive models.

A minor form of automation which can be a great boon is the installation within the greenhouse of suitably spaced spray nozzles. These nozzles are very fine and can create a perfect atmosphere, but of course cannot be used in the winter months. Similarly, a pipe beneath the plants, on the dummy staging which should be inclined inwards towards the walls of the greenhouse, perforated carefully and joined up to the main supply through a cock which can be adjusted so that the water trickles at the right speed—all this will enable you to keep the atmosphere of the house moist with a minimum of work. I do not know yet of an ideal shading system which is fully automatic, but undoubtedly these will come into being as it has already been successfully experimented with by amateurs in Britain and in the USA.

If the greenhouse is a fairly large one, it pays to have a small half or quarter horse power water pump which can be connected to a light hose pipe with an automatic nozzle drawing the water from a rain water tank. This makes watering a very simple and quick job, and saves the lifting of a heavy can of water from the ground level to above pot level.

Epidendrum radicans

These tables will, we hope, be of use, but they should be referred to after the general advice or notes or descriptions have been carefully read. It should be remembered that in nearly every genus some members contrast in some way to the majority, hence the best guide is the study of the plant.

Under 'shading' we have given a few hints for special kinds, but 'see page 28' merely indicates normal shading. The composts, too, may be varied slightly.

Key to alphabetical table of the most Popular Orchid Genera

S—stove.
I—intermediate.
C—cool.
Su—Summer.
A—Autumn.

W—Winter.
Sp—Spring.
p.28—See page 28 for greater detail, etc.
var.—various.

Genus	Greenhouse Division (see p. 21)	Flowering	Shading	Compost (see p. 38 & 39)	Winter Treatment and Specific Notes
ACACALLIS	S	Su & A	From all sunlight	2	Never really rest, but water carefully in winter. Moist atmosphere
ACAMPE	S & I	Su & A	p.28	6	Infrequent winter waterings. for Vanda suavis.
ACANTHO- PHIPPIUM	S & I	Sp	p.28	1 & 4 in equal parts	Rest in Intermediate House.
ACROCHÆNE	S & I	var.	p.28	2	Decided rest in Intermediate House
ACINETA	S & I	Sp	p.28	1	Decided rest in Intermediate House. Does best suspended from rafter
ACROPERA .... (Syn GONGORA)	I	Sp	p. 28	2	Decided rest in Intermediate House. Does best suspended from rafter
ACRIOPSIS	I	Su	p. 28	2	Decided rest in Intermediate House.
ADA	C	Sp	as for Odonts pp. 59–60	3	As for Odontoglossum crispum, avoid moisture in young growths.
ÆRANTHES	S	Su	From all sunlight	6	Careful watering, moist atmosphere throughout.
ÆRIDES	S	var.	p. 28	6	Let compost get moderately dry between waterings. Spray aerial roots whenever possible. See Vandas.
AGANISIA	S	Su	From all sunlight	2	As for Acacallis.
ANCISTRO- CHILUS	S	Su	p. 28	2	Dry moderately in winter, expose to light in autumn.
ANGRAECUM	S	var.	p. 28	6	Water carefully and differentiate between the small and large growing. No decided rest, much as for Vanda.

TABLE OF POPULAR GENERA

Genus	Greenhouse Division (see p. 21)	Flowering	Shading	Compost (see p. 38 & 39)	Winter Treatment and Specific Notes
NGULOA	I	Sp & Su	Light shade p. 28	1 & 4 in equal parts	Never syringe leaves. Remove to Cool House for winter rest.
NŒCTOCHILUS ..	S		From all sunlight	3	Usually succeed better under a bell-glass, avoid draughts, water carefully in winter.
NSELLA	S & I	var.	p. 28	1 with little loam fibre	A decided rest in Intermediate House when growths are made up.
RACHNANTHE ... (Syn. ARACHNIS)	S	var.	p. 28	6	As for *Vanda suavis*.
RPOPHYLLUM ...	I	Su	p. 28	1	Give a decidedly dry winter rest and expose to full light in autumn.
RUNDINA	S & I	Su	p. 28	1 with little loam fibre	Water infrequently in winter but do not dry compost too aridly.
PASIA	C	Sp	p. 28	2	Treat as *Odont. crispum* (p. 60) but slightly higher temperature.
TEMANNIA	S to [	Sp	From sunlight until autumn	2	Infrequent waterings in winter remove to Intermediate House in late autumn.
FRENARIA	I to C	W & Sp	p. 28	1	As for Anguloa, decided rest in Cool House. Moderately dry in winter.
ETIA	I	Su & A	p. 28	5	Decided waterless rest.
ETILLA	C or cool frame	Su	p. 28	5	Rest, but do not dry severely.
NATEA	C or I	Su or A	p. 28	5	Deciduous, decided rest.
RASSAVOLA	I	var.	As much indirect light as possible	1	Decided rest.
RASSIA		Sp. & var.	p. 28	1	Should not be decidedly rested as they are seldom dormant.
ROUGHTONIA ...	S to I	Su & var.	As much indirect light as possible	1	Admit full light in autumn and give decided rest. Are usually grown better on blocks of Osmunda or or rafts, suspended.
JLBOPHYLLUM .	S or I		p. 28	2	Differentiate between the different habits of growths. Those with hard bulbs require rest, others must be watered throughout the year. A very variable genus.
ALANTHE	S	W & Sp	p. 51 Maximum light in winter	see page 53	For the evergreen section use compost 5 and give a short dry rest. See page 53.
ATASETUM	S or I	var.	ditto	1 & 5 mixed	Suspend near glass when resting, water carefully throughout the growing season, and give a thorough rest dry in winter.
ATTLEYA	I or S	var.	pp. 28 & 52	1	Rest with occasional waterings through the winter when dormant. See page 52.
HONDROR- HYNCHA	I	var.	Protect from direct sun and strong light	2 and little loam fibre	Must never be allowed to become very dry.

165

Genus	Greenhouse Division (see p. 21)	Flowering	Shading	Compost (see p. 38 & 39)	Winter Treatment and Specific Notes
CHYSIS	S to I	Sp	p. 28	1 or 3 with little loam fibre	Water infrequently during winter and rest in Intermediate House.
CIRRHÆA	S	Su & A	p. 28	2	Suspend near glass, and water infrequently during winter.
CIRRHOPETALUM .					As for Bulbophyllum.
CLEISOSTOMA	S	var.	p.28		As for Ærides, Vandas, etc.
COCHLIODA	C	W & Sp	As for Odonts pp. 59–60		As for Odontoglossum crispum.
COELIA	C	Su & A	p. 28		C. macrostachya requires a more decided rest than the other species.
COELOGYNE	C & I & S	var.	p. 28	1	A varied genus. Corrugata, corymbosa, Dayana, elata, nervosa, ocellata, ochracea, Rhodeana, tomentosa, require a decided rest in their respective divisions. Cristata benefits by withholding water during December. Smaller growing species rest only one month.
COLAX	C	Sp	p. 28	5	Avoid use of syringe at all times, treat as for Odont. crispum, but water less frequently in winter.
COMPARETTIA	S	Sp & Su	p. 28	2	Usually grow better in small pans or on rafts suspended near glass. Water carefully in winter.
CORYANTHES	S to I	Sp & Su	Light shade p. 28	1 with little more sphagnum	Treat as for Catasetums, but water more frequently in winter.
CRYPTO- PHORANTHUS	C	W & var.	as for Odonts p. 60	3	Treatment as for Odontoglossum crispum. Never dry right out.
CYCNOCHES	S	Su	p. 28	1 & 5	As for Catasetums.
CYMBIDIUM	C	W & Sp	Fairly heavy in summer, expose in autumn see p.55	4	See page 55. Eburneum, erythrostylum and other warmer growing species should not be allowed to fall below 55° F, (13° C) in winter.
CYNORCHIS	I or S	W	Heavy during growth	5	Suspend near the glass and give a decided rest after the leaves fall.
CYRTOPODIUM ...	S to I	Sp	p. 28	4	May be rested in Intermediate House after growth is completed. Expose to light in autumn and winter.
DENDROBIUM	C or I or S	Sp	pp. 28 & 60	1	See pages 59–60. Most enjoy decided winter rest.
EPIDENDRUM	C & I & S	var.	p. 28	1	A varied genus. The hard-bulbed species require a decided winter rest. Small growing soft-bulbed kinds and those with tall reedy stems must be carefully watered throughout the year.

Genus	Greenhouse Division (see p. 21)	Flowering	Shading	Compost (see p. 38 & 39)	Winter Treatment and Specific Notes
ERIA	I or S	var.	p. 28	1 or 2	Allied to Dendrobiums and requiring similar culture, but the majority should be wintered in the division ascribed to them and not dried right out.
EULOPHIELLA	S	Sp & Su	From all sunlight	3	From their straggling habit are better placed on rafts. A moist atmosphere must be maintained throughout the year with a minimum temperature never below 65° F, (18° C)
GOMEZA	C or I	Sp & W	p. 28	2	Treatment as for *Odontoglossum crispum*. (p. 60)
GONGORA	S & I	Su & var.	p. 28	2	In winter allow the compost to become nearly dry between waterings.
HABENARIA	I	ditto	p. 28	3 & 5 equal parts	Give a decided dry rest after the leaves fall, in the division ascribed to them.
HOULLETIA	S or I	ditto	p. 28	2	As for Gongoras.
LAELIA	C & I		pp. 28 & 52	1	As for Cattleyas, but more light in early autumn. *L. anceps* and its allies require a decided rest in the cool division after flowering. *L. pumila* and *monophylla* should never be really dried out.
LYCASTE	C	W & Sp	Light shade p. 28	5	Never syringe leaves. Top air is beneficial whenever safe. Rest after growth is completed, but do not dry to aridity.
MASDEVALLIA	C	var.	Heavy shade p. 28	2	Pseudo-bulbless. They must be kept moist throughout the year. General treatment as for *Odontoglossum crispum*. (p. 60)
MAXILLARIA	C	W & var.	p. 28	2	Judgement must be used. The hard-bulbed species, e.g., *picta*, are the better for a rest with considerable intervals between waterings. Others, e.g., *venusta*, must be carefully watered throughout the winter.
MEGACLINIUM ...	S	var.	p. 28	2	As for Bulbopyllums.
MICROSTYLIS	S		p. 28	3, with a little loam fibre	Deciduous, the plants require a decided but warm rest in the winter.
MILTONIA	I & S	var.	pp. 28 & 58–59	2	Vexillaria and its hybrids are the most popular. Best culture is attained in a Cattleya or Cypripedium house. See page 60.

Genus	Greenhouse Division (see p. 21)	Flowering	Shading	Compost (see p. 38 & 39)	Winter Treatment and Specific Notes
MORMODES	S	var.	p. 28	1 & 5 mixed	Treatment as for Catasetums.
OCTOMERIA	C	W & var.	p. 28	2	Treatment as for *Odontglossum crispum*. Species with fleshy leaves should be watered frequently in winter.
ODONTOGLOSSUM	C	W & var.	pp. 28 & 60	2	See page 60.
ONCIDIUM	C & I & S		p. 28	1 & 2	Read the notes for Odontoglossum. Rest the hard-bulbed or thick leaved kinds in their respective divisions. Such forms as *O. pulchellum*, *O. flexuosum*, etc., usually in growth, must be carefully watered throughout the winter season.
ORNITHIDIUM	C or I	var.	p. 28	2	Treatment as for *Maxillaria venusta*.
PAPHINIA	S	var.	p. 28	2	Suspended near glass. Water carefully in winter.
PAPHIOPEDILUM ..	C or I or S	W & var.	Fairly heavy in summer, less in winter see p. 50	3 & 4	The various species and hybrids must be placed in their necessary divisions. Water is never withheld, but compost must never be waterlogged.
PERISTERIA	S	Su	p. 28	5	After the pseudo bulb is completed give a hard, if necessary, grueling rest to ensure flowering. Plenty of late summer direct light.
PHAIUS	S & I	Sp & Su	p. 28	5	Avoid syringing the foliage. When the foliage becomes shabby in late autumn, remove the *grandifolius* section to Intermediate House or division and water sparingly. The species from Madagasgar require special warm treatment.
PHALAENOPSIS	S	var.	Heavily p. 63	6	Pans or baskets are preferable to pots. The plants are impatient of disturbance and whenever possible remove the old compost and insert new in spring and, if necessary, in early autumn. Avoid the syringe in winter. Water must be given in winter but with care, avoiding leaves.
PHOLIDOTA	I	var.	p. 28	2	As for Dendrobiums.
PHRAGMIPEDIUM .	I & S	var.	p. 28	5	As for Cypripediums.
PHYSOSIPHON	S	W	p. 28	2	As for *Odontoglossum crispum* (p.60) but never dry out.
PLATYCLINUS	S		p. 28	2	Suspend near the glass, water carefully in the winter, allowing the compost to become moderately dry between waterings.

168

Genus	Greenhouse Division (see p. 21)	Flowering	Shading	Compost (see p. 38 & 39)	Winter Treatment and Specific Notes
EIONE	C	W & Sp	Fairly heavy	5	Avoid syringing and re-pot annually directly after flowering. Water very carefully. Rest in winter, giving very occasional waterings, if any. Is deciduous
EUROTHALLIS ..	C	W & Sp	Shade heavily p. 28	2	Treat as *Odoent. crispum* (p. 60). The species with fleshy foliage requires less frequent waterings than the thin-leaved forms, but never allow to dry out.
OLYSTACHYA	I	var.	p. 28	2	As for Dendrobiums, but rest in their respective divisions and water infrequently in winter.
ENANTHERA	S & I	Sp & Su	p. 28	6	As for Ærides.
ESTREPIA	C	W & var.	p. 28	2	Treatment as for Pleurothallis.
HYNCOSTYLIS ...	S	Su	p. 28	6	As for Ærides.
ODRIGUEZIA	S	Su	p. 28	2	Pans or rafts are preferable. Suspend the plants near the glass. Water throughout the year with discretion in winter.
ACCOLABIUM	S	Su	p. 28	6	As for Ærides.
ARCANTHUS		Su	p. 28	2	As for Ærides.
ARCOCHILUS	I & S	var.	p. 28	2	As for Ærides.
CAPHOSEPALUM .	C	var.	p. 28	2	As for *Odont. crispum.* (p. 60)
CHOMBURGKIA ..	I	Su	p. 28	1	As for Cattleyas, but dry out in winter. Page 52.
CUTICARIA	I	Su	p. 28	2	*S. steeli* succeeds better on a block as the leaves are pendant. Both species should be rested in winter but avoid shrivelling the leaves.
OBRALIA	I & C	Su	p. 28	5	Can often be grown in Cool House, but should be rested in Intermediate division in winter. Water should be given but not too frequently. Avoid disturbing roots when potting.
OPHRONITIS	C	W	p. 28	3	Grow in the Odont. House but water infrequently for a short period after growths are finished. Shade heavily.
PATHOGLOTTIS ..	S	Su & A	p. 28	5	Give rest, but occasional winter waterings are required.
TANHOPEA		var.	p. 28	1	The flower spikes are descending, hence baskets should be used and suspended near the glass. Rest in winter but give occasional waterings do not allow water to remain on the young foliage.
TELIS	C	var.	Shade heavily p. 28	2	As for Pleurothallis. Never dry out.

Genus	Greenhouse Division (see p. 21)	Flowering	Shading	Compost (see p. 38 & 39)	Winter Treatment and Specific No
STENOGLOTTIS	C	A	p. 28	5	Deciduous. Rest in winter, wa ing very seldom if at all, di and re-pot in early March required. Heavy summ shading.
THUNIA	S & C	Su	Shade lightly in Summer	5	Give as much heat and moistur possible when growing. W freely. Rest in Cool House. K dry. Re-pot in March.
TRIAS	S	A	p. 28	2	Treatment as for Bulbophyllu
TRICHOPILIA	I & C	Sp & Su	p. 28	1	Treatment as for Cattleyas, rest in their respective divisi Pans are preferable to pots can be suspended.
TRICHOSMA	C	W	p. 28	2	Treat as *Odont. crispum*. (pp. 59
VANDA	S & C	Su & A	pp. 27 & 61	6	*V. suavis* and its allies must watered throughout the year, not too frequently in win Allow the compost to moderately dry. *V. kimball* and *amesiana* require v infrequent waterings as d *V. coerulea* after the flower time. Spray regularly except cold winter days.
VANILLA	S	var.	p. 28	6	Can be trained on a trellis or wires on the roof.
ZYGOPETALUM ...	I & S	var.	p. 28	6	The bulbous section, e.g., *mackayi*, should be potted No. 6 compost; they can grown with *Odontogloss crispum* but are the better fo temperature of 58°F, (15° minimum during winter.
				3	The bulbless section require No compost and must be wate throughout the year, and sho be carefully shaded duri bright weather.

REFERENCES

Some of the earlier books of interest are:

Blowers, J. W.	London 1962	*Orchids.*
Blowers, J. W.	London 1967	*Pictorial Orchid Growing.*
Cox, J. Murray	Sydney 1946	*A Cultural Table of Orchidaceous Plants.*
Curtis, Charles H.	London 1910	*Orchids for Everyone.* 234 pp. illus.
Darwin, Charles R.	London 1903	*Fertilization of Orchids.* 300 pp. illus.
Davies, R. and Steiner M. L.	N.Y. 1952	*Phillipine Orchids.*
Dunsterville, G. C. and Garay, L. A.	London 1961/2	*Orchids of Venezuela. Vol. I (in 4 parts.)*
Grubb, Roy	London 1961	*Selected Orchidaceous Plants.* (hand printed collectors series: 6 parts)
Lecoufle, Marcel	1957	*Orchidées.* 150 pp. illus. English translation.
Logan and Cosper	1951	*Orchids are Easy to Grow.*
Northern, Rebecca	N.Y. 1962	*Home Orchid Growing.*
Piers, Frank	Nairobi 1968	*Orchids of East Africa.*
Sander, David F.	London 1961/2	*One Table List of Orchid Hybrids.* (2 vols.).
Sanders	1927	*Orchid Guide.* 256 pp.
Sanders Orchid Hybrid List	1955	Collated List of Orchid Hybrids complete to 1954 inclusive.
Schlechter, R.	1914	*Die Orchideen,* well illustrated, over 550 pp.—in German.
Swinson, Arthur	London 1969	*Frederick Sander—the Orchid King.*
Thomale, Hans	1954	*Die Orchideen.* 100 pp.—in German.
Vacherot, Maurice	1954	*Les Orchidées.*
Veitch, James & Sons	1887	*Manual of Orchidaceous Plants.* (2 vols.) illus.
Watkins, John V.	1947	*A.B.C. of Orchid Growing.*
Watson, Wm.	1903 (reprint Amsterdam 1963)	*Orchids: Their Culture and Management.* 559 pp. illus.
White, Ed. A.	1947	*American Orchid Culture.*
Williams, B. Samuel	1894 (reprint 1961)	*Orchid Growers Manual.* 796 pp. illus.
Willoughby, Adelaide C.	1950	*Orchids and How to Grow Them.*
Withner, Carl L.	N.Y. 1959	*The Orchids, a Scientific Survey.*
Wright, N. Pelham	Mexico 1958	*Orchideas de Mexico.* English translation.

Books on orchids continue to appear but the following periodicals are of special interest:

The Orchid Review. The oldest Orchid Journal (monthly), dating from 1893.

The American Orchid Society Bulletin. A first class monthly Orchid Journal started in 1932.

The Gardener's Chronicle. A weekly paper with excellent cultural notes. Founded in 1841.

The Cymbidium News and Orchid Digest. Two Californian monthlies.

The Australian Orchid Review. A quarterly illustrated journal.

The Malayan Orchid Review. A quarterly illustrated journal.

Die Orchidee. The excellent monthly journal of the German Orchid Society (in German, illustrated).

Transvaal Orchid Society Bulletin. Published monthly.

AERIAL (roots) ....Peculiar to tree loving orchids; feeding on the atmosphere as opposed to the earth.

ALBINO ....The white variety of a species or hybrid (often yellow or green).

APICAL ....Pertaining to the top or apex of bulb.

ARIDITY ....Dryness of atmosphere.

ASPECT (of a greenhouse) ....The lay of the house relative to the north, a hill, a wood, dwelling-house, the sea, etc., etc.

ASYMBIOTIC ....Without artificial stimulation of growth by use of fungii.

AUTOMATIC (sprayer) ....Atomises water by pressure of air.

AXIL ....The delicate juncture of leaf and bulb or leaf and stem.

BACK-BULB ....The oldest bulb of the plant, usually leafless.

BOTTOM-AIR ....Ventilation under the staging.

BRACT ....Refers to the abortive leaves that sheaf the bulbs and new growths of orchids.

BULB ....See pseudo-bulb.

BUOYANT (atmosphere) ....Lively, fresh, not overheated nor overmoist air.

CLEISTOGAMIC ....Self-fertilising flowers which therfore rarely expand.

CLONE ....A variety, but of a hybrid (cross).

COLUMN ....The central (sexual) body of the orchid flower.

COMPOST ....A mixture of fibres, moss, leaves, loam, etc., making up food for the orchids to root in.

CONNATE ....Joined together.

CORIACEOUS ....Leathery, usually thick.

CROCKS ....Broken up brick.

CRUSTACEANS ....Snails (having shells).

DAMPING (down) ....A process of wetting all parts of the house below plant level.

DECIDUOUS ....Loosing its leaves annually.

DEHISCING ....Breaking apart; splitting.

DIANDROUS ....Having two stamens, *e.g.*, Paphiopedilum.

DIPODIAL ....Breaking into two or more lateral horizontal growths.

DISTICHOUS ....Set alternately and closely together along the stem.

DORMANT (season) ....A resting period when the plant hibernates (usually with no water) and does not grow.

DUMMY-STAGE ....A second stage below that on which the plants are placed and above the pipes.

ELEVATION ....Height above sea-level.

EPIPHYTE ....Tree loving, clinging to trees, but not necessarily parasitic.

EXOTIC ....Foreign, not native to country.

EYE-BUD ....Dormant new growth.

FLACCIDITY (of leaves) ....A visible weakening and drooping.

FLESHY (of leaves) ....Thick, and soft, loose-celled.

GENERA ....Plural of genus.

GENUS ....A family or branch of related orchid species.

GROWTHS ....That portion of the plant leading; the newest, youngest bulb or leaves in formation.

HYBRID(ISING) ....The cross or 'child' resulting from the act of fertilising one flower with the pollen of another.

HYDROPONIC ....Soil-less culture in liquid or neutral medium *(e.g.,* gravel) impregnated regularly with liquid.

HOMOGENEOUSLY (of potting) Uniformly, smoothly, in such a manner as to bind the compost together into one root ball.

INDIGENOUS ....Native to country, not exotic.

INFLORESCENCE ....The flower spike and its arrangement.

LABELLUM (lip) ....The third or lowermost petal, always the most striking in colour and shape.

LATERAL ....Pertaining to the sides—on either side.

LEADS (leading bulbs) ....The result of a new growth fully developed, and in front, as opposed to *back* bulbs.

LOAM-FIBRE ....Rich fibrous, fatty loam sifted free of the smaller particles of earth.

MERISTEM ....Anescent growth of embryonic proportions.

MONANDROUS ....Having one stamen, *e.g.,* Cattleya.

MONOPODIAL ....Growing only from the apex of plant.

MOTTLED (leafed) ....Marbled, paler on darker green.

MULTIGENERIC ....Referring to orchid hybrids of more than two genera.

NATURAL (of heating) ....Sun-given or atmosphere heat as provided by Nature.

NEEDLE ....Knitting (bone or metal) for seedlings and of platinum when used in laboratory handling seed and plantules.

NODAL (point) ....A point where young new growths appear, usually sheathed.

OSMUNDA ....*O. regalis* and *cinnamomea* are species of ferns whose roots are known as 'Osmunda', used in composts for orchids.

OVARY ....That part of the pedicel in which the seed is formed.

OVER-POT ....To pot in *too* large a receptacle (a common malpractice).

PANS (Orchid pans) ....Broader-than-deep pots, usually freely perforated at sides and base.

PEDICEL ....The apparent stalk of the individual flower.

PENDANT ....Sloping downwards.

PERIANTH ....The six parts of the flower known as petals, sepals and lip.

PETAL ....One of the three inner segments of the perianth of an orchid flower.

p.H. ....A scale for measuring acidity and alkalanity.

PLACENTA ....The adhesive matter at the base of the caudicle attaching pollinea to the column.

PLANTULE (plantlet) ....A minute orchid, fresh from embryonic stage, 1 to 5 mms.

PLICATE (leafed) ....Flat, broad leaves of a mackintosh texture (like an aspidestra leaf).

POLYMORPHIC ....Very variable in form.

POTTING-*ON* ....As opposed to *re-*potting, consists of moving a root ball into a larger spaced pot and filling in from the front with fresh compost.

POTTING-STICK ....A carefully graded smooth, apiculate but rounded teak or oak stick, 8/12 in. long and ½/¾ in. thick.

PSEUDO-BULB ....A false bulb, and forming above ground-level.

RE-POTTING .:......................The removal of the old compost, and replacement by a larger quantity of fresh.

RESTING ....The period at the end of the growth cycle when the water is withheld because the plant is not growing new leaves/bulbs.

RHIZOME ....A woody stem that creeps along the ground or pot surface, from which bulbs and leaves rise.

RIPENING ....Maturing; hardening off; exposing to more light and air, and less water and heat.

ROOT-ACTION ....The lively root system, growing, lengthening, taking food and moisture.

SCANDENT ....Climbing, needing a support.
SCORCHING ....Burning of foliage by the sun, magnified by moisture in the air, bubbles in the glass, or drops on the leaves.
SEEDLING ....A young orchid plant from 6 months to 6 years old.
SEMI-TERRESTRIAL ....Growing naturally on debris such as fallen trees or rocks.
SEPAL ....One of the three outer segments of the orchid flower.
SHADING ....The covering of glass with permanent wash or lathes or blinds.
SHEATH ....The protective membranes that enclose the flower spike during its early stages, usually at the top of the bulb or growth.
SHEATHING MEMBRANES ..A protecting (against sun) skin found around parts of leaves and bulbs.
SOFT-BULBED ....As opposed to a hard resistant woody bulb. (Some orchids never rest long enough to harden the new bulb.)
SPECIES ....One distinct plant type within a genus.
SPECIMEN ....In the sense of a fine large plant, *e.g.*, a Cattleya with 20 bulbs and 5 leads.
SPHAGNUM ....A bog-moss.
SPIKE (in spike) ....The flowering stem about to flower.
STIPPLING ....The spreading of a whitish (summer cloud) in mottled fashion, dabbed or streaked over the glass intermittently.
STRAGGLING (habit) ....With untidy rhizomes which branch out, around, and even upwards.
SURFACING ....Cleaning off the top compost from around a plant and replacing with fresh; filling in the gaps.
SYMBIOTIC ....Covering the relationship between an orchid plant and a living matter (fungus).
SYRINGING ....As opposed to spraying, a coarse jet of water forcibly expelled and spread with the finger.

TERETE (leafed) ....Pencil-thin leafed, usually pointed.
TERRESTRIAL ....Truly growing on the ground.
TOMENTOSE ....Having a hairy surface.
TUBEROUS (rooted) ....Truly forming root swellings shaped like tubers, just beneath the surface.

UMBEL ....Having a cluster of flowers springing from the same point.

VANDACEOUS ....Monopodial type, that is, growing *up*wards vertically, as oppposed to rhizoctomous plants growing horizontally *along*.
VARIETY ....One of many forms a species may take by slight or greater variations from the type, *e.g.,* albino.
VIRUS ....A little understood disease, which rarely kills but spoils the leaves with moisaic-like markings.
VISCOUS ....Refers to the sticky stigmatic surface at top of the column below the pollen cap.

WETTABLE (solution) ....One which mixes with water.

XEROPHITIC ....Drought loving; desert conditions.

ZYGOMORPHIC ....Refers to those hybrids made between two distinct species which reproduce however only the genes of the one dominant parent, *e.g.,* Zygocastes.

174